Library of
Davidson College

EXPERIMENT IN UNITY

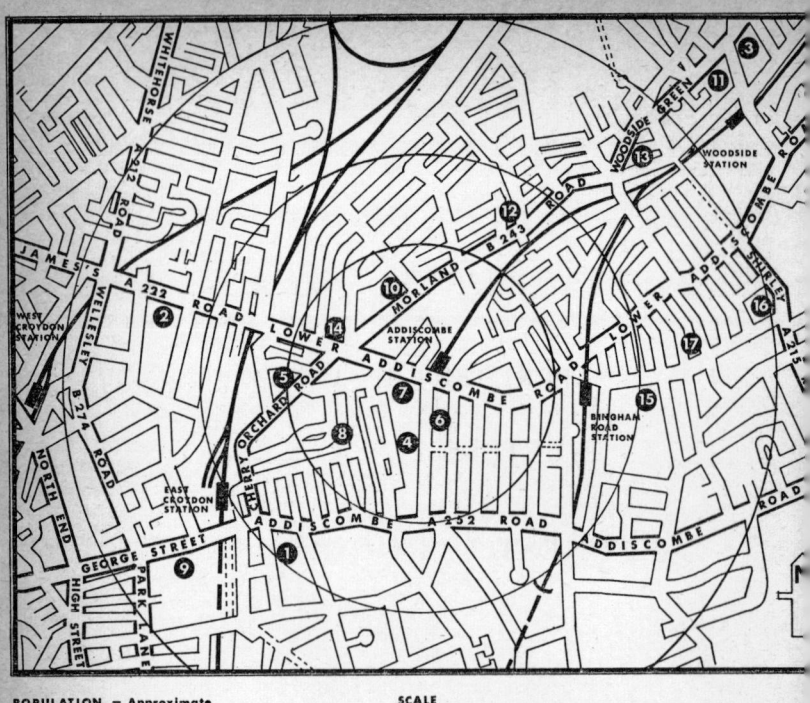

POPULATION — Approximate	
1811 — East of East Croydon Station	200
1891 — " " " " "	10,000
1967 — inner circle	12,000
middle circle	24,000
outer circle	48,000

MAP OF THE ADDISCOMBE AREA—*London Borough of Croydon* showing disposition of church premises referred to in the text and approximate populations within the radius of the Parish Church of St. Mary Magdalene and Addiscombe Methodist Church.

1. George Street Congregational 1765 (Addiscombe Grove 1964)
2. St. James 1829
3. St. Luke 1850
4. St. Mary Magdalene 1868 (Consecration 1878)
5. Cherry Orchard Methodist Hall 1870 —Church 1884
6. Christ Church Congregational 1880–1957
7. Addiscombe Methodist 1881
8. Oval Mission Hall 1885 (St. Mary Magdalene)
9. St. Matthew 1886
10. St. Martin's Hall 1889—Church 19
11. Woodside Baptist 1898
12. Addiscombe Baptist 1901
13. Woodside Methodist 1910–1943 (Adventist 1948)
14. Holiness Mission 1912 (Church of the Nazerene 1953)
15. St. Mildred's Hall 1913—Church 1
16. Roman Catholic Hall 1925—Ch 1964
17. Christian Brethren 1932 (former St. Mildred's Hall)

EXPERIMENT IN UNITY

An account of joint action between churches in an Urban area

by
NEVILLE B. CRYER
and
ERNEST N. GOODRIDGE

LONDON
A. R. MOWBRAY & CO LTD

© *A. R. Mowbray & Co Ltd 1968*

*Printed in Great Britain at
the Pitman Press, Bath*

SBN 264 65558 3

First published in 1968

CONTENTS

Foreword	*page* vii
Introduction	xi
1. The Addiscombe Setting	1
2. In Principle and Practice	15
3. In the Home	29
4. In the Road	45
5. In the Church	64
6. In with Others	86
7. In Conference	105
8. In Colleagueship	129
9. In Worship	143
10. In the Future	155
Appendices	163

ACKNOWLEDGEMENTS

THE thanks of the author and publishers are due to the following for permission to quote extracts:

The Baptist Union, *Baptists and Unity;* The British Council of Churches, *In Each Place, The Lund Conference on Faith and Order,* 1952 and *Second Ecumenical Work Book;* The Clinical Theology Association, *The Pastoral Ministry Today;* Epworth Press, *The Early Church and the Coming Great Church* by John Knox.

Foreword

By The Bishop of Croydon

At fairly frequent intervals sermons are preached and articles are written to tell us what the Church ought to be doing, not merely in a general sort of way, but often in quite practical detail. Not infrequently this comes across to us as only another version of the constant stream of criticism both from within and from outside itself to which the Church is nowadays subjected. I do not quarrel with the contention that the Church needs criticism and can never safely do without it for long. But what I have often thought is this: I wish someone would sometimes tell me, not what he thinks *ought* to be done for the revival of the Church, but what in fact he himself *has* done. A page of testimony is worth a volume of exhortation.

Particularly today. It is easy both for the clergy and the laity (especially the clergy) to feel discouraged. It would be foolish and irresponsible to question the need for the recognition of new areas of pastoral opportunity and of new kinds of 'specialist' ministries to serve them. But what of the ordinary locality in which people normally live, where their homes and families are—the locality which is served by its local government with various social services at its disposal, and which is contained within a 'parish' and a 'district' of local churches with their clergy and congregations? There is a tendency nowadays to write these off as unproductive and 'unexciting' because they are superseded by something better.

This book has been written to tell us what has happened over the past few years in an area of Croydon. This is what a handful of clergymen, Anglican and Methodist principally, but including also a Roman Catholic priest, and their congregations, have been led to do together, with the ministry committed to them by our Lord, with all kinds of other resources, some obvious, others less immediately so, amongst the people, the problems, the needs and the opportunities which they found precisely where they were. The centre of a man's gravity is where he is at the present moment said Dietrich Bonhoeffer. 'The Church in Addiscombe' has been changing its form over the years because Christians who live in Addiscombe have been making *discoveries:* because they have been alive and alert to see and to hear what God has been opening out before them in Addiscombe. And those discoveries have been as much about themselves as about anybody or anything else.

They have had to look, to listen, and to learn. But they have succeeded in doing all these because they have been willing to act. No-one gave any of them any kind of blue-print. What happened happened because over the years men and women saw signs because they were looking, and because they then became committed in risk to what they believed they saw. Of course they made mistakes, but that did not surprise or deter them. That is part of the process of learning for those who believe in not only the leading, but also the redeeming power, of the Holy Spirit.

Although all this has been taking place on my doorstep as it were, much of the story in this book is new to me. I have of course known many of the people concerned, some of them intimately, and I have been acquainted generally and sometimes in detail with what has been going on, even occasionally becoming directly involved in it. But the story behind the story—this thrilling and moving story—I have not heard before. Perhaps had I been more enquiring than I was, I might have known it. The fact is that by not asking the questions I could have asked I have not known it. And the principal reason is that those who were committed to what was taking place were not concerned with making a story or having one to tell. They had no eye on any likely audience. They were hard at work, getting on with the job they believed they were being required by God to do.

But now something of what has been taking place has been simply, honestly and factually set down in these pages. What I already knew and what I now know in greater depth and detail I believe to be an authentic illustration of much that Lund 1952, Evanston 1954 and Nottingham 1964 have been expecting to take place, and what in one way and another will have to take place if the Churches are to discover a living unity and then to continue in it. If this is a right appraisal of the Addiscombe experiments, then this story is indispensable and we shall have to receive it seriously. What are the factors which make this kind of experience possible? What does it cost? If we give ourselves to asking such questions as these and to finding the right answers, we shall be making the right use of these pages. They contain no blue print for anyone. The Churches in Addiscombe are where they are only by the way they came, and that way is their own. What they have to commend to us is a spirit and a method.

This is a book of great encouragement, and I am honoured and delighted to recommend it to all who believe in the coming unity of the Church and who are determined to work for it.

JOHN CROYDON

Introduction

REMARKABLY few detailed accounts are yet available of what has actually happened when a group of churches starts practical experimenting in unity. In this book we have described, as factually and honestly as we can, an experiment which has become an experience of unity. It is not a 'success' story; it is simply an attempt to provide what a great number of Christians seem to be asking for: someone else's experience to work on, someone else's methods and material to use, emend or reject. It has been a surprise to discover how many seem unable to push out the ecumenical boat beyond the familiar limits of co-operation, for want of some clue as to how others have set about it.

In 'A Second Ecumenical Work Book'[1] there occurs the following passage: 'Picture four new ministers . . . arriving in quick succession, and meeting week by week, almost from the start, to pray and plan together for their common "mission field" with its four congregations, in the conviction that they must do nothing separately that CAN be done together. Picture them calling a kind of *ad hoc* church council (drawn from the P.C.C., Leaders' Meeting and Diaconates) to share with them month by month in this praying and planning. Picture next, this council involving the four congregations in a new partnership based upon the roads in which they live, and upon the local factories in which most of the breadwinners work. Picture the comprehensive visitation carried out by these road-and-house groups; picture them being mobilised as action-groups (including some Roman Catholic households) for neighbourly service; picture some of them learning to pray and

[1] See Bibliography.

to study the Bible together in their homes. . . . Picture the congregations learning in a measure to worship together; witnessing together a parish eucharist, a believer's baptism, a Methodist covenant service; sharing with some regularity in each other's liturgical traditions; making the same solemn and joyful pilgrimage through the Christian Year. Picture them more and more pooling their "family life", in weeknight activities, in their service of children and young people, in their training of members. Picture them active TOGETHER in the social and civic life of the town, with a common parish newspaper going into every home. . . .'

This is not a precise description of Addiscombe, but we have had the inestimable privilege of experiencing something like it.

We wish to thank the publishers for their encouragement and patience, and the leaders and members of our several congregations without whom there would have been no 'experiment' at all. We acknowledge with special gratitude the work of our predecessors in the ministry and thank those who have permitted us to quote from their writings and experience. (We have, incidentally, included some of the basic data of the ecumenical movement—particularly from the Nottingham Report[2] but there is also some 'ready made' material here, such as the three Conference outlines, for those who wish to use it.) Our story is largely concerned with the three-and-a-half years of our own Anglican-Methodist colleagueship, but we have also tried to indicate the nature of earlier and subsequent developments. It is a matter of particular significance that when our colleagueship came to an end in 1967 with Neville's departure for another sphere of ecumenical work, lay patrons made an appointment which would ensure continuity of policy within an acknowledged 'area of ecumenical experiment'. Since, however, we are personally involved in the greater part of this story,

[2] *Unity Begins at Home*, S.C.M. 1964, 3/6. Popular report of the first British Faith and Order Conference.

we may be forgiven, at this point, a personal confession. For Neville the real hope and power of the ecumenical movement in the local church began when, fourteen years ago, he knelt down with four other Anglican laymen and five Methodist people in the local manse. For Ernest the same conviction was given in 1949 at the Ecumenical Institute, Bossey, when sixty students from twenty countries discerned their unity in Christ across the deep divides of the second World War.

We record our indebtedness to Miss Dorothy Cornwall (Group Organiser of the Addiscombe Churches), Miss Muriel King (Group Secretary) and Mrs. Peggy Wallis (Vicar's Secretary) as well as those other church members who have generously assisted us with the typescript. Not least, we acknowledge the help and understanding of our wives and families upon whose love and loyalty this book has been an added imposition. Finally, we thank God for bringing us, the authors, together 'in one place' so that we might draw upon each other's gifts and go on our ways the richer for sharing an 'Experiment in Unity'.

1. The Addiscombe Setting

'ADDISCOMBE Place' or 'Addiscombe House', as the local 'big house' was variously known, is recorded as occupied by men of some substance from the fifteenth century onwards. Amongst others, the House was occupied by John Evelyn's son-in-law and a reference appears in Evelyn's Diary for 13 March 1700. However, the fortunes of the House have no direct bearing upon the present London suburb until 1808, when the Estate was sold by the then owner (Henry Delme, Master of the Stud to George IV) to the East India Company for use as a training establishment for their cadets. Hitherto they had received instruction at Woolwich but, as the 'supply of officers for the more scientific arms was insufficient, and, owing to the continuance of the French War, uncertain, the Court of Directors came to the determination of having a Military Academy of their own. In 1809 this Academy at Addiscombe began and fifty-eight students started the honourable line of soldiers, statesmen and administrators whose effect on the life and history of India cannot be underestimated.'[1] An incidental cutting from Tait's *Magazine* for 1860 will give just one contemporary view of the work done at the College. Commending a new 'History of British India' the critic writes, 'A more valuable present than the volume before us could not have been offered for those youths who are now qualifying at Addiscombe and Haileybury to eclipse the glories of a Clive, a Hastings or a Wellesley.' Amongst those youths were Stewart, the pioneer of military telegraphy, Sir Henry Lawrence, Lord Napier and Lord Roberts. The commandant of the College was emphatically a person of consequence in local society and when his stepfather

[1] *Millenary Booklet*, Addiscombe Chamber of Commerce, 1961.

at one time occupied that position the novelist, William Makepeace Thackeray, used to spend his vacations in the district.

The estate naturally began to change even during the Company's tenancy. Various buildings were constructed round the central mansion and one of these is still in existence—the hall used for exercising the horses in inclement weather—now a warehouse for an electrical equipment firm. The road to which this hall is attached bears the name of Havelock, and this too is the road in which the vicarage for St. Mary Magdelene's church now stands. The Methodist manse is in the next road running parallel to it—Elgin Road—and the names of other thoroughfares all around (Outram Road, Grant Road, Warren Road, Hastings Road and Clyde Road) indicate clearly the historical associations to which we have already alluded. One road perhaps links the past and the present even more intimately. Almost opposite St. Mary's vicarage is one of the latest streets with its pleasant semi-detached houses. It is called Mulberry Lane, for at one end of the line along which this sideroad runs there once stood an enormous mulberry tree—a feature of the original estate which was well-known to some of the present inhabitants until just before the last World War.

The advent of the College and its cadets also affected the growth and form of the Addiscombe neighbourhood. At first the cadets marched on Sundays across two miles of estate, though the main street of the town and down the hill to the Croydon Parish Church on the west side of the Borough. By 1829, however, it was clear that a further 'chapel of ease' was needed to serve the Academy and there thus appeared the present parish church of St. James, much less than half the distance from the Addiscombe estate. The cadets and their instructors' families brought more trade to the district and when to these developments you add the coming of the horse tram, the making of better roadways and the need of a growing industrial Croydon

THE ADDISCOMBE SETTING

for more residential areas to the east—the direction of Addiscombe—it can easily be seen how what had hitherto been a very rural adjunct to a distinctive country town started to change into the suburb that it has now become. Until the mid-nineteenth century the story of Addiscombe is the story of its large houses (Ashburton Estate was the other property), their families and servants and a few small farms. In this it differed only in degree from the history of most of the rest of our predominantly rural society up to that time. That was now to change. The old fairs, like the Cherry Fair in the orchards on the way to Croydon, and the annual Horse Fair held on a site near the top of the Havelock Road already mentioned, both vanished—though we still have Cherry Orchard Road and a Methodist Society which also bears that name. The conversion of fields to roads and the coming of large Victorian houses, which in their turn are now fast disappearing, is linked with the creation of the new parishes that appeared in this part of East Croydon. St. James' chapel became a full parish in 1853; St. Mary Magdalene's, Addiscombe, was built in 1868; St. Luke's, Woodside, in 1871 and two 'missions' followed, St. Martin's in 1889 and finally St. Mildred's, 1913.

Yet the most sweeping changes in the locality were those that occurred when the British Government had assumed all the responsibilities hitherto exercised in India by the East India Company. The War Office then considered that its own establishments could accommodate all the personnel involved and Addiscombe College was sold. The estate was immediately broken up, the house razed to the ground and the last main memorial of the link between Addiscombe and the 'Hon. John Company' was effaced. A couple of pleasant Victorian houses, one of them with an almost Indian-style verandah, still grace the turning from Clyde Road to the South; these were the earlier residences of tutorial staff who taught at and therefore lived well within the grounds of the older college. Apart from these and a house still called—but in no way resembling—Addiscombe Farm, the outward scene has entirely changed, indeed almost doubly changed, since those days when the 'sons of Empire' were trained in this neighbourhood. Perhaps it was of set purpose that those who gave the present roads their Indian associations chose the names of persons who had never actually been members of the local college!

Since then the character of Addiscombe has remained much the same. Situated as it is within easy access of fast trains to central London as well as the coast at Brighton it has proved to be a residential area of great convenience. Within the area with which this book deals, an area of about two miles square, there have since been only two significant alterations in its make-up. The first was the shift in the 1930s when the large detached houses and the imposing four-storey terraces of the late-Victorian suburb began to be converted into flats or were demolished and replaced. The second shift is at the present time when large modern blocks of Corporation flats have begun to appear, as well as a great many private and more costly residential flats, detached and semi-detached 'town-houses'. These serve the new commuting population which needs rapid access to the City but prefers to live in more congenial surroundings than are often obtainable in the intervening districts (Brixton, Streatham, Thornton Heath or Selhurst).

This is not to suggest that Addiscombe is made up mainly of city-workers' families though many in the higher-income brackets are in that group. Of the middle-class families who live in the terraced houses or flats it can be fairly said that most of them regard their present accommodation as of only temporary significance and a turn-over of 10% of the population annually is as normal here as in most other parts of the South London area. In addition, the continuing presence of the lofty and unmanageable Victorian terraced property has provided

THE ADDISCOMBE SETTING

homes for a growing West Indian population—a factor to which the churches here have had to give their attention and to which later reference will be made. Full and steady employment in this area has thus meant for all the residents these two things—high prices and much competition for what property becomes available, and the wish of many to be able to afford even more pleasant, or owner-occupied, properties a mile or two further from the train or town-centre.

Cars abound and the parking meters which have inundated inner Croydon begin to appear in the Addiscombe thoroughfares. There is no industry to speak of and even the shopping centres are clustered together so that the residential character of the area has been retained. In many ways it is still a new community, about 45,000 in number, covering three Anglican parishes, St. Mary Magdalene's, St. Martin's and St. Mildred's (and parts of others), two Methodist Churches, Addiscombe and Cherry Orchard, and stretching farther afield, the Roman Catholic parishes of West Croydon and Addiscombe which converge in Canning Road, where St. Mary Magdalene's church stands. Other Christian bodies will be mentioned as the story proceeds.

Yet even though the meadows of the past are now submerged under bricks and mortar, Addiscombe does not present that featureless uniformity that can often be seen in some other areas of South London. The reactions of its inhabitants have been treated imaginatively by R. F. Delderfield in his two-volume work, *The Avenue Story*, and R. J. Minney and D. H. Lawrence both had associations with the area, thus giving it a note of literary distinction.[2] It is not for nothing that one of the most successful open gatherings on church premises in Addiscombe is the Literary Society held in the Museum Hall

[2] See especially *The Trespasser* by D. H. Lawrence. (This book describes an actual occurrence whilst the author was a school teacher in the area.)

of St. Mildred's. Started in 1932 by the Rev. Dr. Budden, the second Vicar of the parish newly-carved-out of the older St. Mary's, this Society has flourished, war in, war out, ever since. Mention of the birth of St. Mildred's, however, leads us on to the background and history of the churches with whose common life this book is seeking to deal. There are some very interesting facets here.[3]

The Victorian age in Britain was one in which volumes of sermons were 'best-sellers' and the utterances of the great preaching divines were the topic of much polite conversation. It was the desire to have a 'worthy preacher' of their own that prompted the Anglican inhabitants of the new residences erected on the Addiscombe House estate to demand by 1867 that something better than a mission hall of St. James should now be provided. Meeting in the old 'riding school' mentioned earlier was hardly what our wealthy ancestors regarded as proper, and an association was formed to construct a suitable edifice in Canning Road, using an otherwise unknown architect for the purpose.[4] They also approached the curate at another Croydon church, St. Matthew's, to be their first incumbent but this move was firmly opposed by the Vicar of St. James'. The young man in question, however—the Rev. Maxwell Macluff Ben Oliel—a converted Rabbi and the offspring of a Jewish father and a Scottish mother—declared himself ready to accept the invitation and duly prepared to officiate at the new church. Though the Archbishop of Canterbury, the Diocesan, felt himself unable to consecrate a building erected without episcopal sanction Ben Oliel, still only a deacon (*sic*), was unabashed and proceeded to dedicate the church himself. He named it after St. Paul, his eminent predecessor, and being like him a gifted

---

[3] Fuller treatment is given in *Addiscombe Parish Church; Its History and Jubilee*, Rev. J. Wright. 1927.

[4] See *Surrey*. Ian Nairne and Nikolaus Pevsner. The Buildings of England Series. Penguin 1962.

linguist, an erudite scholar and a powerful preacher, Ben Oliel's ministry flourished. The fact that there has since his day been almost no ecclesiastical endowment here only typifies the solid support given by the residents of Addiscombe in the past century to the work of their local churches.

The story of the following years, especially after the swing of Ben Oliel from Evangelical to Anglo-Catholic churchmanship, has been told elsewhere and cannot be repeated here. The fact remains that by the year 1874 the church had been re-named St. Mary Magdalene's and is so known today. Official recognition of the new parish was duly obtained and the congregation which had forsaken Oliel in the interim came back again in large measure under the new Vicar, Henry Glover, another ex-curate of St. Matthew's. He was to serve them for the next forty years! It is still puzzling to visitors to see a stone set in the East Wall marking the consecration as being in 1878 when they also learn that the present building had been in existence for ten years previously.

From the time of the Rev. Henry Glover onwards the life of St. Mary Magdalene's has been a fairly steady one. Together with the next Vicar, Mr Wright, the parish had only one change of incumbent in seventy-five years. Meanwhile the neighbouring parish of St. Mildred's began to take shape. In 1911–12 some three hundred and fifty houses had been erected on the Ashburton estate to the east and, as there was no place of worship of any kind, the Church of England Men's Society members met and rented the Gordon Hall for a year with the curate of St. Mary Magdalene's as Curate-in-Charge.[5] In 1922 the Hall ceased to be the Chapel of Ease that it had become and in 1932, under the vigorous leadership of the Rev. Charles Budden, the present church building and main organisation of St. Mildred's parish was launched. The full story of this

---

[5] This Hall is now used by the Christian Brethren.

growth has also been told elsewhere[6] and we are sensible of the thriving contribution that St. Mildred's is still making to our common church life and ecumenical development. As we know it today this comparatively young parish is something of a religious phenomenon, for something around one-third of the houses are found to have some active Church association. By present-day standards St. Mildred's is strong and immensely alive. But the full religious strength of this parish is not reflected in the parish church; upwards of a dozen churches in Croydon owe much of their leadership to this one.

Alongside these developing Anglican churches the Methodist Societies were also establishing themselves in the Addiscombe area. Three years after the opening of the 'free' Anglican church of St. Paul's, the Wesleyan Methodists secured a site in what was then the St. James' Road 'after prolonged negotiations with the trustees of the church at Addiscombe lately occupied by the Rev. Ben Oliel'.[7] The name of the unorthodox Mr. Ben Oliel thus provides a first link between the Anglican and Methodist churches here. Eight years later, in 1878, the Croydon Directory indicates that there were 'Services on Sundays, morning and evening, and on Thursdays at 7.30 p.m. Baptisms Sunday mornings and *Thursdays* at 7.30 p.m. *Church of England Liturgy* used at Sunday morning services' (our italics). The weeknight baptisms are indicative of the growing population following the sale of the Addiscombe College in 1860 and the development of the land between the Lower and (Upper) Addiscombe roads for building purposes. In 1881 the original 'iron' building used by the Methodists was replaced by a spired church in stone, built on an 'Anglican'

---

[6] See *The Story of St. Mildred's, Addiscombe* by Rev. Charles W. Budden and R. R. Hutchinson. Croydon, 1937.

Also *Parishes with a Purpose* by N. B. Cryer, Mowbrays 1967, pp. 15–26, for the more up-to-date story.

[7] Minutes of the Quarterly meeting, Croydon Circuit, 27 December 1869.

THE ADDISCOMBE SETTING

cruciform pattern, with chancel, transepts and side pulpit. The 'Croydon and County Pictorial' of 1905 describes a church where monthly People's Services, followed by a social, trebled the normal congregation, a P.S.A.[8] with its own string band attracted 200 people a week, and activities included 'slate' clubs[9], Mothers' Meetings, Penny Bank, and a Dispensary. Some Methodist families moving into the area in the early 1900s, faced with a 'Prayer Book' service confessed that only loyalty to Methodism held them; some may have felt more at home in the small daughter chapel which operated from 1910 to 1943 at Woodside. The church, however, had its typical nonconformist opinion, and there was considerable criticism when the Rev. Leonard Hale (1930–33) invited Dr. Budden, Vicar of St. Mildred's, to preach in the Methodist pulpit, and later, when in the time of the Rev. George Cottrell (1943–52) a wooden cross was placed on the Lord's Table. In 1931, Addiscombe Methodists had given birth to a daughter church at Shirley, the next district to the east, and a hundred members of the old society provided the nucleus of the new.

The Methodist premises were almost entirely destroyed by fire in January 1948. For two-and-a-half years worship was held in the Congregationalist Hall in Clyde Road. The Methodists then moved into what had been their former church hall, now a simple rectangular sanctuary dominated by a life-size oak cross and a richly embroidered table frontal. The Communion chalice and the alms dish were the gifts of St. Mildred's and St. Mary Magdalene's respectively—the two parish churches with which the Methodists were most closely associated.

The Cherry Orchard Methodist Society was formed during a vigorous period of Primitive Methodist missionary expansion,

[8] 'Pleasant Sunday Afternoon'.
[9] Voluntary 'Friendly' Societies for insurance against unemployment and illness.

the first preaching service being held in 'old Granny Cornfield's cottage' in Cross Road. In 1870 the 'Iron Room' was purchased as a temporary chapel and at the same time a piece of land in Cherry Orchard Road was acquired. The opening of the present premises, on the new site, came at the end of 1884 and 'brought our work to one of the main roads of Croydon'.[10] It was hoped that a membership of eighty-seven would double within twelve months. The opening Public Meeting, held on Boxing Day under the chairmanship of Mr. J. S. Balfour, M.P., J.P., was notable for the reflections of the Church Secretary, Mr. H. J. Allen. 'I maintain,' he said, 'that politics and religion are more closely associated than we are apt to imagine . . . I hold that Primitive Methodism today is greatly indebted to the Liberal Party.'[11] The great benefits of Liberalism ('free speech, free schools, free trade, free press and a free Bible'[12]) were still much in the minds of the Primitive Methodists when they celebrated their Jubilee in Croydon in 1900. By this time Cherry Orchard had the largest Sunday School in a circuit extending as far as Sutton, Streatham, South Norwood and Thornton Heath.

The Jubilee celebrations of the Society, held in 1935, two years after Methodist Church Union, provided an opportunity for assessment: 'True to the best Primitive Methodist traditions, the Church was thoroughly evangelical, lively in its worship, evangelistic in its spirit. In addition to the preaching of the Word, prayer meetings, love feasts, and open-air services were the order of the day, whilst the Sunday School grew in strength, at one time numbering more than 200 scholars.' If the first World War had seen the departure of the Drum and Fife band and the Saturday night Prayer meeting, the Junior and Senior sections of the Christian Endeavour remained and

[10] Primitive Methodist Croydon Circuit Jubilee Brochure 1900.
[11] *Croydon Advertiser and Surrey Reporter*, 3 January 1965.
[12] *Ibid.*

were soon joined by a flourishing Women's Own and Men's Institute. The Youth Club work, begun during World War II, became a joint activity with the nearby ex-Wesleyan society from 1956–66 but has since continued to operate independently. The Sunday School and Choir represent notable traditions in the life of the Church, the latter being one of the strongest in Croydon.

In what is now an area of high-density population and geographically small parishes worshippers have long been accustomed to cross parish boundaries to the church of their choice. Thus our two neighbouring Anglican congregations, no less than the Methodist, are drawn in part from outside the immediately surrounding district. The work we describe has in consequence touched the life of several other parishes, including St. James and St. Matthew's, St. Martin's and St. Luke's, Woodside (to all of which some passing reference has necessarily been made). The coming of St. Luke's into the more direct fellowship of the Addiscombe churches in 1965 brought us into close association with the Anglo-Catholic tradition.

In the immediately post-war years the Congregational Church in Canning Road (opposite St. Mary Magdalene's) was an active partner in local church life, but with its closure in 1957 our associations have been limited to friendship with churches which were more naturally linked in other directions. Apart from the small Addiscombe Baptist Church our Baptist association has similarly been with Baptists who were sited on the fringe of our 'working area'. However, Church cooperation, if pioneered by Anglican-Methodist relationship, has not been confined to that 'axis'. Links have been forged with the Christian Brethren, with the 'Church of the Nazarene'—an independent Mission of post-war origin—and, most recently, with the Addiscombe Roman Catholic Church, Our Lady of the Annunciation. For many years Addiscombe Roman Catholics worshipped at a temporary church on the Lower Addiscombe Road but increasing numbers necessitated a much larger building and this was opened in Bingham Road in 1964. The friendship of the priest there, Fr. John McKenna, and his people, has been one of the notable features of latter-day church life in Addiscombe and the Catholic-sponsored 'Unity Club' has been one of the most significant of our ecumenical breakthroughs.[13]

Our story, then, is set against a typical backcloth of varied origins and traditions. Here is no unnatural uniformity of outlook or conviction. The viewpoints represented here could find their parallels in many other areas of Britain. But, undoubtedly, the impetus to church unity in our area has been provided largely by a steadily-developing Anglican-Methodist colleagueship.[14]

During the period from 1949 and on the basis of the happy personal relationships existing between the Rev. John Girling of St. Mildred's and the Rev. George Cottrell of Addiscombe Methodist Church in particular, we can already note the emergence of several ecumenical engagements which were pointers to the work of the future. The 1949 'United Campaign' brought together five churches in a Mission. In 1949–50 we read of a 'Flying Squad' operation in which teams of young people from all the denominations in Croydon were commissioned to visit youth clubs as witnesses for Christ, to hold open-air meetings and to engage in special types of visiting. Later, House Groups were anticipated; Mr. Cottrell and Mr. Girling were joint leaders in this evangelistic venture and Addiscombe was given the chance to share its growing ecumenical experience with the rest of the Borough.

In April 1950, the Anglicans at St. Mildred's, the Methodists and the Congregationalists at Christ Church, Canning Road

[13] See Chapter 5, page 74.
[14] See Chapter 8.

held their Holy Week services as a United act and this was followed in May by the Anniversary weekend of the United Campaign. By now St. Mary Magdalene's had once again become involved and as the weekday meetings had been held at St. Mildred's, it was at St. Mary's that the united Sunday evening services took place. The hospitality offered by the other churches to the Methodists during these years, 1948-50, when they had no place of worship of their own, was not without significance for the growth of church fellowship.

Perhaps this panorama of earlier relationships can best be summed up by a short comment from the St. Mildred's magazine of November 1950, in which there is printed an extensive and friendly account of the dedication of the reopened Methodist premises. The writer described the Methodist Church as the 'home of friends' and spoke later of how the welcome extended to their neighbours on this occasion witnessed 'yet again to the unity of the church in Addiscombe'. As we have been heartened to discover in making these researches we were not, in 1965, as some of the present generation may have imagined, the first to describe ourselves as 'The Church in Addiscombe'.

Because this book must centre mainly on events immediately known to us we cannot pursue in too much detail the years between 1950 and 1963. What we need to do is to recall that all through this period the ecumenical experience and outlook was preserved. The United Men's Forum, first conceived in the Joint Mission of 1949, a joint Holy Week service on at least one day in that octave, an occasional Anglo-Methodist retreat, as in 1951, and the willingness to have regular exchanges of preachers at other times in the year—all these acts continued to be a part of the local situation and led to the formation of a separate Addiscombe and Shirley Council of Churches, thus bringing Addiscombe into valuable association with a neighbouring area. What was also not without significance was that the intervening ministries of the Rev. (now Rt. Rev.) Gordon Strutt at St. Mary's and of the Rev. Dr. Hollinghurst at the Addiscombe Methodist Church led to a strengthening of their respective congregations and their being better informed in the faith—an essential preparation for those who were later to be engaged in house-meeting encounter or who were to hold out the hand of fellowship again to their Christian neighbours.

Meanwhile, in Manchester and Bicester, the authors were already engaged in similar kinds of ecumenical relationship. One of us came from an upper working class area north of a large industrial zone; the other from the compact and more distinct community life of a country town. Both of us, however, were from the same generation of theological students, eager to encourage in the local church the sense that all of us in the 'church-body' were meant to be 'the Church' wherever we went and whatever we did in work or worship. Both of us had the desire to make our worship meaningful for those who attended it and were concerned to enlist the full cooperation of everyone qualified to relate life and liturgy. Both of us were aware that unless we, the Church, lifted up our eyes and looked beyond our own walls, beyond our denominational landmarks, beyond even our own common Christian concerns, and out onto the 'fields' which lay all around us, we were bound to lose the vision of the Church as we believed that God meant us to portray it. For both of us, therefore, as we came into partnership in Addiscombe the 'slogan' of Nottingham was a summary of our joint outlook: 'One Church renewed in Mission.'

2. In Principle and Practice

OUR 'working together' between 1963 and 1967 was made possible more by our social and cultural patterns than by the deliberate examination of first principles. Ours was an area in which it was not difficult for the leadership of the respective churches to establish relationships of mutual respect. It was late in the day, when much had already been done together, that the necessity of an overall commitment became apparent, and then it was only entered into *formally* by two churches. The work we describe in the following chapters came as the response of the churches to what seemed required of them by God in a given set of circumstances. This seems to us a realistic method of proceeding: obedience at one point has illuminated for us God's purpose at another. We have found that principle and practice are mutually dependent. Nowhere has this been more apparent than in the inter-church Home Fellowships: obedience at the point of fellowship was the *sine qua non* of other discoveries, not least that 'our remaining differences . . . can be better explored within a united Church'.[1] Nevertheless, we became aware of dangers: a succession of detailed decisions, each seemingly right in the circumstances, was committing the churches to a policy and direction which had not necessarily been assessed and approved as a whole. In particular, we felt that the biblical background was insufficiently explored and understood. The following heads may serve to indicate the significance we attach to some of the biblical material:

The Creation of Man-kind and the fruit of the first enmities

[1] Nottingham Resolutions, Section 1, Resolution 3.

(Gen. 1:3 and 4)—God's Election of Israel (Exod. 19:5, 6, etc.)—twelve tribes yet one people (Deut. 33)—condemnation of disloyal tribes (Judg. 5: 15–17) and the sin of civil war (1 Kgs. 12:21–4)—Prophecy of the reconciliation of Israel and Judah (Jer. 3:18)—purification and centralisation of the Worship in Jerusalem (2 Kgs. 23:1–15)—Prophecy of the re-gathering of the scattered flock (Ezek. 34, etc.) and of Zion the religious and legislative centre for all nations (Isa. 2:1–4).

The Birth and Baptism of Jesus (Matt. 1 and 3)—the Confession of Jesus as Israel's Messiah (Matt. 16:13–16)—the Call of twelve to re-form Israel (Matt. 10:1–7, and see Luke 22:29–30) —the Announcement of the New Worship (John 4:19–26) and of the New Law (Matt. 5–7)—the establishment of the New Covenant between God and his people (Mark 14:22–5, etc.)— teaching of the one Flock (John 10:7–16) and Prayer 'that they may be one' (John 17: 20–23).

The unity of the first Christian believers (Acts 1:14; 2:46; 4:32)—the account of God's dealings with a People (Acts 7: 2–53)—incorporation of the non-Jew into the Divine Commonwealth (Eph. 2:11–14)—reconciliation of Jewish and Gentile Churches (Acts 15)—message of the New Humanity, Household, Temple (Eph. 2:15–22), Body (1 Cor. 12:12–27) informed by the one Spirit (Eph. 2:22, etc.). The sacraments of Baptism (Gal. 3:26–8) and Communion (1 Cor. 10:16–17) as sacraments of incorporation into the divine Unity. Unity not broken by diversity (1 Cor. 12:4, etc.), conscientious difference (Rom. 14:7 and 13–15; also 1 Cor. 10:23–33) or even factiousness (Phil. 1:15–18). The Church as a new Race, Priesthood, Nation and People (1 Pet. 2:9–10) with a Message of Reconciliation (2 Cor. 5:17–19) which anticipates the reconciled community of Heaven (Rom. 8:18–21; Rev. 7:1–10).

Among summary statements of the biblical material we have been impressed by the section 'Biblical and Theological Principles concerning the Unity of the Church' in the Report

Baptists and Unity.[2] On the biblical evidence the Report concludes that 'The total redemptive ministry of the Lord was concerned with the People of God . . . The entire process of this once-for-all redemption of the Saviour was directed to the creation of the people of the Kingdom. To introduce into this set of concepts the thought of a multiplicity of divided churches is as out of place as the idea of a plurality of kingdoms of God, or a profusion of Saviours, or a number of different Gospels. The one Church corresponds to the one Saviour and one salvation . . . Such figures of the Church as the Body of Christ, the Bride of Christ, the Temple of God by the Spirit, the chosen Race, royal Priesthood, holy Nation, people of God's love, all conjoin with the Church the idea of unity, and in such a fashion as to make the concept of alienated Churches inconceivable.'[3]

We do not see how it is possible to hold such a principle of unity without commitment to a practice of unity. We note how principle and practice are brought together in the 'Basis' of the World Council of Churches, agreed at its first Assembly held at Amsterdam in 1948: 'The World Council of Churches is a fellowship of churches which confess the Lord Jesus Christ as God and Saviour according to the Scriptures *and therefore* seek to fulfil *together* their common calling to the glory of the one God, Father, Son, and Holy Spirit.'[4] (The italics are our own.) The World Council of Churches does not claim that the Basis is a Confession of Faith, but here, at least, is an affirmation of the Lordship, Messiahship, Divinity and Saviourhood of Jesus, and by these terms, interpreted 'according to the

---

[2] The Report prepared by the Advisory Committee for Church Relations of the Baptist Union of Great Britain and Ireland. See also *The Bible and Unity*, R. E. Davies, pub. B.C.C., and *Visible Unity—What Does the Bible Say?*, J. M. Ross, pub. Friends of Reunion.

[3] The Report prepared by the Advisory Committee for Church Relations of the Baptist Union of Great Britain and Ireland, pp. 40–1.

[4] *Questions and Answers—About the World Council of Churches*, W.C.C. Obtainable from B.C.C.

Scriptures', we see the Churches bound to an understanding of themselves as the one, stubborn but redeemed, People of God. The inescapable conclusion is that, within this faith no 'church' is free to withold recognition of the other any more than a man can deny kinship to his mother, brother or child. The attempt to evade this conclusion by implying that the 'other' church means an entirely different thing by the same confession of faith, does not, we believe, bear sympathetic examination and denies to the Christian Faith any meaningful terms of reference. The seeing of the life of the churches in each place as a whole, and the recognition of the other church as a part of it, we understand to be the basic working principles of the ecumenical movement.

The principle of 'recognition' implies the preparedness to 'work together'. The point is made in the Baptist Report in these terms: 'The thrust of the (Apostolic) exhortation (Eph. 4:3) should not be turned by asserting that the unity of the Church is "spiritual". We must avoid the peril of making "spiritual" mean "ineffectual". The operation of the Spirit is unseen, but its effects are intended to be evident . . . The realities of the Church's unity . . . surely demand that some effort be made to embody them in the empirical life of the Church . . .'[5]; The declaration of the Third Assembly of the World Council of Churches, at New Delhi in 1961, was more explicit: 'In some things our convictions do not yet permit us to act together . . . Let us therefore find out the things which in each place we can *do together* now and faithfully do them, praying and working always for that fuller unity which Christ wills for his Church.'[6] The principle had been stressed at the Lund Conference on Faith and Order, 1952, and was spelt out by the first British Conference on Faith and Order held at Nottingham in September 1964. The resolution unanimously

[5] *Baptists and Unity*, pp. 44 and 48.
[6] *Questions and Answers—About the World Council of Churches.*

IN PRINCIPLE AND PRACTICE

passed under section five, part B, has become a basic working-document of the search for unity 'In Each Place': 'Recognising that visible unity will only be realised as we learn to do things together both as individuals and as congregations, this Conference invites the member Churches of the British Council of Churches to implement the Lund call to "act together in all matters except those in which deep differences of conviction compel them to act separately". In particular it invites them:

'1. To make every effort to promote the common use of church buildings and to set up whatever machinery is necessary to implement this';

'2. To declare that the following activities should be carried out jointly or (where this is not possible through deep reasons of conscience) coordinated, namely: 'learning together' including local ecumenical study conferences and Faith and Order groups, lay training, youth work, children's work, men's and women's organisations, local church publications, Christian Aid, programmes of visiting, concern for and service to the whole life of the local and wider community;

'3. To designate areas of ecumenical experiment, at the request of local congregations, or in new towns and housing areas. In such areas there should be experiments in ecumenical group ministries, in the sharing of buildings and equipment, and in the development of mission.'

In the chapters which follow, the reader will gain an impression of the things we have done, in our own situation, to put this resolution into practice. It will be evident that, though our circumstances may be regarded as extraordinarily favourable, we have done no more than make a beginning. For the remainder of this chapter we enunciate certain additional working principles which have particular reference to the less 'favourable' aspects of each local situation. These may be placed under the following heads:

1. *Recognition of non-cooperating churches as within the*

ecumenical venture.[7] We believe that the onus is on the 'convinced' church to prove the integrity of its conviction by the fullest possible recognition of the church at present unable to accept the claims of the ecumenical movement. Attitudes within the early Judaeo-Christian Church towards the Gentile mission have their counterpart within the life of the Church in the mid-twentieth century, and require of us the honesty and the charity of a Barnabas and a Paul.[8] Following an invitation addressed to the Minister of the 'Church of the Nazarene' in Addiscombe, the ministers of the local Group of Churches received a reply which included the following paragraph: 'We hold Scriptural, doctrinal and ethical standards which we cannot surrender, compromise nor besmirch. From statements uttered publicly by some of you—some via the press; by activities allowed and promoted on your church premises; and because of the denominational standards represented by one of your group, we feel there is no basis for union. . . .' We believed that New Testament principle and practice required of us respect for traditions more exclusive and legalistic than our own, and we sought to express this by continuing to provide material and information of common interest. 'Non-cooperating' ministers have been notified of the House Visiting and information has been forwarded to them where applicable. Information about their church activities has been included in the Road Warden files. The principle of courtesy—even where sympathies are tightly stretched—keeps open a line of communication, modifies the rigid position and preserves a fundamental principle of unity.

2. *Recognition of churches not fully committed.* Ernest's second church, Cherry Orchard Methodist, is a notable

---

[7] See also B.C.C. Statement March 1966 on *Covenanting Together to Work and Pray for Union*: 'Any standing out from the commitment asked for shall be respected on both sides as being still within and part of a common open commitment to God's will for his people.'

[8] Acts 15; Gal. 2.

illustration of the point we wish to make here. A Primitive Methodist foundation, the Society, though much changed since Methodist Church Union (1932), has maintained a strong tradition of lay responsibility and family association. As one of the five members of the early Addiscombe Council of Churches, it had experience in the immediate post-war years of working with its sister church, Addiscombe Methodist, together with the Church of England and the (then) Addiscombe Congregational Church. From 1956 to 1966 it gave hospitality to the joint Methodist Youth Club, was one of the three churches involved in the Anglican-Methodist Men's Forum 1954 to 1967, and one of the six churches which sponsored the inter-church 'Abbeyfield' House project in 1965 to provide homes for the elderly. In the preparation of the first 'Abbeyfield' House, Cherry Orchard's contribution of voluntary labour was out of all proportion to its numerical strength. In 1964 it made the difficult and generous decision to offer the hospitality of its premises to the 'Church of God', a West Indian Pentecostal group. Yet in May 1966, when the Leaders and Trustees were invited to follow the example of their immediate neighbours and commit themselves to a simple 'Lund' covenant, they were unable to do so. The reasons were not far to seek: In 1959 the mother church at Laud Street was closed, leaving Cherry Orchard the sole surviving link with Primitive Methodism in central Croydon. In the years which followed, uncertainty about its own future was created by its 'transfer' to the Croydon, South Norwood, Circuit in 1955, the loss of its 'own' minister, and a proposal presented to the Trustees in 1955 to sell. In the succeeding decade the Society was deeply sensitive of anything that appeared to threaten its own name and existence, and in 1966, when the development of the Youth work as an Anglican-Methodist venture was being contemplated, it closed its premises to the open Club and commenced Youth work of its own. It is a commonplace of ecumenical work that many churches, with much to offer, will be 'out' of the engagement unless, at the beginning, there is respect for their distinctive life as free and equal partners. One of the most difficult lessons we have learned is to accept—for the time being—the position of those churches which, for various reasons, seriously advanced, still believe that it is required of them to develop some of their work along denominational lines.

3. *Acknowledgement of the contribution to the life of the Church of the 'dissentient' view.* We have tried to believe that we have something to learn from those who are not willing to cooperate with us as far as we would wish—or at all. In its statement of March 1966 on 'Covenanting Together' the B.C.C. emphasised the principle of inclusion, rather than exclusion, and calls attention to 'churches and bodies . . . which feel called to witness to some other features of churchly life which they hold to be at least as important as, or even more important than, visible unity'. As we see it, the dissentient view derives from two fears, usually bound together; the fear of losing an identity and the fear of betraying a standard. We have attempted to treat both fears seriously and believe that they may have something to say to us. Over against the obvious claims of centralisation, concentration, rationalisation, etc., the former fear presents the claims of preservation, dispersion and diversity. Is a congregation of five hundred necessarily a more effective unit of Christian Worship and Witness than a congregation of fifty? Are the small premises necessarily made redundant by the presence of larger? We are inclined to put the 'ideal' size of congregation at 200–300, but we dare not assert that a much smaller congregation, with a distinct life and tradition, has no place within the context of churches seeking unity. We think we have experienced our full share of unhappiness at the spectacle of churches professing allegiance to a crucified Lord and dedicated to their own self-preservation;

but we know that we cannot wholly disassociate ourselves from the shame. We suspect that the type of leadership which we represent has itself helped to create the threatening situation within which the local church has been involuntarily thrown back to the defence of its own name and dignity. Disconcertingly, the biblical concept of Israel presupposes the distinctive existence of the tribe within the life of the whole People.

We have already quoted a minister whose fear was said to be that of betraying a standard. The evidence of tension, both doctrinal and ethical, within the New Testament Church, the recurrent 'holiness' movements of Church History, and, above all, the self-conscious 'evangelical' position represented throughout the churches at the present time, persuade us to approach our critics with attentiveness and humility. If we are saddened by the limits of their charity, we are humbled by their faith and hope. Though it has been necessary for us, in our 'epistles' to the Home Fellowships, to warn our people against extreme positions—Pentecostalist, Adventist, and Anti-nomian —we believe that a total withdrawal of the 'central' church traditions from the difficult boundary area of Church and Sect may prove to be a betrayal of the purpose of unity at its most critical breaking-point. The exercise of mere courtesy serves, at least, to keep some relationship open. The minister who wrote declining our invitation to share in the Addiscombe Group of Churches Visiting work did not want us 'to assume that we are snobbish or isolationist' and submitted his church's decision 'humbly and without rancour'. We felt that these assurances implied some recognition of the claims of Christian unity. In general, we sympathise with the Baptists and others who are said to remain 'unconvinced that adequate attention has been given to the practical as well as the theoretical problems of avoiding uniformity and rightly relating diversity to unity'.[9]

[9] *Baptists and Unity*, p. 21. And see Bibliography, *Baptists For Unity*.

4. *Preparedness for the perpetuation of earlier attitudes into the new situation.* Within a situation of commitment—as between the Addiscombe Parish Church and the Addiscombe Methodist Church in Addiscombe—it is not to be expected that habits of mind are changed overnight. The 'ours–theirs' conception of church premises and activities has not yet worked itself out of our system and has been one of the problems facing us in the creation of the inter-church Community Centre on Methodist premises. Some Methodist support was probably lost when it was discovered that Wednesday was no longer 'ours'. Anglican support has been difficult to rally, in part, because the venture appeared to be 'theirs'. Fair questions have been asked on both 'sides' about finance: at a Methodist Leaders' Meeting it was asked whether the Anglicans were proposing to contribute to the maintenance of Methodist premises when in use for joint activities. The answer was that this and allied matters were being kept under review by the ministers and their advisory committees and that there were other factors to be taken into account—particularly the Anglican provision of premises for the joint Youth Work and the support to the life of the whole Church given by a Church Army Captain. A sense of humour, much generosity and realistic policy-thinking have all proved essential requirements of the venture.

5. *Preparedness for areas of 'No Progress'.* It will be apparent that in numerous directions we have to report 'no progress'. One example may be in our relationship with the West Indian Pentecostal Group whose request for the hospitality of the Cherry Orchard Methodist premises was granted in 1964. In more typical areas of ecumenical experiment we have had to receive the reports of exploratory committees and accept the likelihood of several months or years of little advance. We have not seen appreciable development of thought regarding wholly united Parish Worship since the principle was generally

accepted that our two congregations (at least) should join for a united Parish and Family service twice each year.[10] Joint Sunday School staff meetings were unable to proceed to much fuller active cooperation, initially through problems of accommodation and timing, but subsequently through difficulties arising from material and method.[11] Until the Anglican-Methodist Church Union scheme is in operation, we do not expect to move far in the rationalising of church finances, though we envisage minor adjustments and major exploration.[12] Again, until 'Stage Two' we expect that premises will continue to be held denominationally, whatever the use to which they are put. However, we have constantly found that matters 'left on the table' have a way of coming alive again within a slowly unfolding situation.

6. *Preparedness for disturbance to existing attitudes and practices.* Obedience to the purpose of unity, where this has been possible, has created a situation in which we have had to be prepared for the continual re-assessment of customary attitudes and practices. The Home Fellowships[13] have produced new basic attitudes between members of one denomination and another, not least between Protestant and Catholic; the Home Mission[14] has introduced a new dimension into the 'routine' life of the churches and begun to transform existing structures of pastoral care and church records. An outstanding example is the way in which the Parish Church of St. Mildred's, with an extensive road warden organisation of many years' standing, has welcomed the help of road wardens of other denominations and remodelled the organisation on an inter-church basis. We have seen the spirit, the objectives and the shape of the churches changing in ways more far-reaching than any envisaged in the original commitments. The introduction of the 'fish' sign[15] was an interesting example of an ecumenical venture challenging

[10] See Chapter 10.   [11] See Chapter 5.   [12] See Chapter 8.
[13] See Chapter 3.   [14] See Chapter 4.   [15] See Chapter 4.

to personal attitudes: in several cases, the appearance of the *ichthus*—say in a Roman Catholic window across the road—has presented a daily challenge to a life-long prejudice. Richard Baxter, as so often, has the judicious comment. Concerning his recommendations to Cromwell's 'Toleration' committee he writes: 'I would have had the brethren to have offered the parliament the Creed, Lord's Prayer and Decalogue alone as our essentials or fundamentals, which at least *containeth all* that is necessary to salvation, and hath been by all the ancient Churches taken for the sum of their religion. And whereas they still said, "A Socinian[16] or a Papist will subscribe all this", I answered them: "So much the better, and so much the fitter it is to be the matter of our concord . . ." '[17]

7. *Preparedness to enter into definite commitment.* We have already indicated that formal commitment to the Lund principle came after years of regular or occasional 'working together' in practice; it was *then* only a commitment between two churches out of a group numbering upwards of twelve. But when the matter was raised in the Parochial Church Council and Leaders' Meeting in the Autumn of 1965, there was almost unanimous agreement on both sides that a policy and direction so long implied should now be formally endorsed and agreed. We recorded the Lund formula in our respective Minutes as the guiding principle of our future work and agreed that the principle was to be interpreted in practice along the lines indicated by the Nottingham Conference. To a point, our commitment was on the basis of what we had known, but we were also committing ourselves to the unknown. The arrangement whereby two observers from the other church were invited to attend all ordinary meetings of P.C.C. and L.M. we now see to have been an essential part of the commitment.

[16] After a sixteenth century Italian religious teacher associated with unitarianism.

[17] *Autobiography of Richard Baxter*, Everyman's Library N. 868, p. 139

This arrangement ensured that there could be no easy disengagement and that in each church all things were now done with an eye to (and under the eye of) the other. This simple arrangement, more than anything else, provided for continuity of policy through changes of incumbents and ministers, and was the pledge that we meant business. We doubt whether a Group or Council of Churches can move effectively towards the goal of unity apart from some such commitment in principle and practice and a preparedness to go to the point of no return.

We have occasionally had what amounts to a request for a 'crash programme' of ecumenical development. It is possible to imagine churches, stabbed into action by the approach of 1980,[18] asking for a five-year plan of action. Such requests cannot be met with a simple formula. No two situations are identical and in each place the varied insights of unity will be given different emphasis and priority. Yet, almost in self-defence, we will dare to set down, from our experience in Addiscombe, what we see as a possible five-year programme.

It is always helpful to one's own thinking to have someone else's ideas to reject:

Year One
Monthly Ministerial groups for study and fellowship.[19]

Year Two
Monthly lay 'pilot' groups for study and fellowship.[20]

Year Three
Monthly Home Fellowships in the pastoral care of the Ministerial staff, involving as many members of the churches as homes and leadership permit.[21] Exploratory meetings of church workers engaged in the same field of service: e.g. Sunday

[18] Nottingham, Section 5, Resolution A 2. See page 78.
[19] See Chapters 3 and 8.
[20] See Chapters 3 and 18.
[21] See Chapter 3.

School, Youth, Adult organisations, Pastoral Care, Service to the Community, Publicity, Finance, etc.[22]

Year Four
Act of Covenant in the terms of 'Lund' and 'Nottingham', with agreement on exchange of observers at principal church councils and one major engagement to a joint activity.[23]

Year Five
Preparation of over-all review of local church resources—manpower, experience, premises, finance—and presentation to the churches of an outline scheme for the establishment of 'The Church in this Place'.

The ensuing pages offer a partial commentary on this outline.

The danger of presenting the principle and practice of unity as a 'programme' is the impression of something imposed upon and not essential to the life of the Church. But unity is the practice of the Divine Presence within the Church. It is no more external to the Church's life than breath to the body. We have seen it as a Breath of the Spirit of God renewing the lives and relationships of Christian men and women, and in others, reviving the hope that Christ may still be found among those who confess him. Our 'programme' at least indicates our priorities: We believe that our first major obedience to the unity of Christ was our return to the 'upper room'[24] and our preparedness to 'see each other's face'.[25] It is here, first, that we found our 'togetherness' and it is therefore with the home that we continue our story.

[22] See Chapters 5 and 8.
[23] See Chapter 2, etc.
[24] Acts 1:12–13.
[25] Charles Wesley, M.H.B. 709.

3. In the Home

THE Methodist Deed of Union stipulates that 'Membership of the Methodist Church . . . involves fellowship', that 'the weekly Class Meeting has from the beginning proved to be the most effective means . . .'[1] In 1963 Addiscombe was typical of British Methodism as a whole: only one Class was meeting, on Church premises. The post-war revival of the Class, apparent in one or two areas of Croydon, had not come our way. But in 1957, Canon Gordon Strutt, now Bishop of Stockport, had shared an 'idea' with the congregation at the Parish Church of St. Mary Magdalene. He talked one Sunday morning about 'transplanting the Church into the home, and calling into being the House Church'. Pastorally he saw this as the place 'where the saints, who are the called of God, can grow in knowledge'; evangelistically it was a place where the saints might 'become aware of need in other people'; practically it was 'good strategy', the establishment of 'a loving community dispersed through this place'. He described the stages by which the House Church might be brought into being and the pattern which an hour of meeting might take. His vision was not fully realised. At the Parochial Church Council Week-end Retreat in April 1961, one group was asked the question: 'Are there any improvements you could suggest for the House Churches as part of our missionary out-reach?' The reply was: 'Not fully discussed'. The vision which Gordon Strutt shared with his people that Sunday morning is probably more convincing after ten years than it was then. He anticipated something

---

[1] *Deed of Union* clause 33, Constitutional Practice and Discipline of the Methodist Church, 1958 (Revised), p. 266.

which was probably not realisable outside an ecumenical setting. Nevertheless, when the present writers became colleagues in 1963, eight House Churches were still in being, sustained by members of St. Mary Magdalene's congregation.

The ecumenical house-group had already been anticipated in Addiscombe during the close colleagueship of the Rev. John B. Girling of St. Mildred's and the Rev. George C. Cotterell of the Addiscombe Methodist Church, from 1948 to 1952. During the summer of 1949 five Addiscombe Churches cooperated in a mission to the neighbourhood, under the leadership of the Vicar of St. Mary Magdalene, the Rev. Harold Frankham. During the ensuing months an inter-denominational 'Christian Witness' team met in various homes twice each month for prayer and study. In the autumn of 1949, John Girling and George Cotterell led a remarkable Anglican Methodist Week-end Retreat near Haslemere. Apprehension was confessed on both sides. 'We returned', said a Methodist member, 'with a sense of thanksgiving and gladness that we belonged to the Church, which is the undivided Body of Christ.' But these were anticipations. Influential in the lives of those who experienced them, these events brought no permanent change to the customary Church life of Addiscombe. The close friendship of two ministers, the drama of the fire which in 1948 gutted the Methodist Church, the still-close memories of war—these pressures in time would cease to operate and the Churches would be left looking very much the same as before. The new impetus of the House Church movement was undoubtedly given by the opening of official Conversations between the Anglican and Methodist Churches and the compulsion to read the Interim report of 1958 and the subsequent Report of 1963. By this time, colleagueship and geography were linking the Methodists with Neville Cryer's Parish of St. Mary Magdalene. The P.C.C. Conference of April 1961 had already agreed in principle (if without great enthusiasm) 'to establish at least one small working-party of six people to meet regularly with a group from the Methodists to thrash out exactly where we stand in regard to them'. Such a group, consisting of four Anglicans and four Methodists (two from each of the two local Methodist Churches) was formed the following year; a second followed in 1963. Led initially by one or other of the two Ministers, Neville Cryer and Frederick Hollinghurst, pilot-groups 'A' and 'B' soon discovered a life of their own. Study was based on the two Reports, and as the groups explored the faith and practice of their respective Churches they grew in mutual respect and understanding. It was one of these groups which one night became a Confessional. Speaking slowly to a member at the other side of the room, an ex-Primitive Methodist said: 'I am ashamed to confess that only a few years ago I didn't believe that a high church Anglican was truly a Christian.' The confession was mutual.

Neville and Fred realised that in the pilot-groups they possessed a potential for something that would go beyond the bounds of the Anglican-Methodist encounter. When Ernest Goodridge succeeded Fred Hollinghurst in September 1963, thought was already being given to the next step. The immediate requirement was that as many of our people as possible should have the opportunity of meeting their 'opposite numbers' in the face-to-face relationship of the small house group. Considerable leadership was already to hand in the pilot-groups and we knew we could count on the help of Lay Readers, Lay Preachers, and others with the requisite experience. But unconsciously we were thinking along the lines suggested by Gordon Strutt in 1957 and seeking to give the groups an objective beyond that of a Church-union scheme. It was generally acknowledged that the eight Anglican House Churches, faithfully maintained, seriously led, had become static in membership and removed from their 'evangelistic' and 'strategic' intention. The Methodists, with the word 'fellowship' often on their lips, presented a no more convincing picture, though numerous groupings in the church offered fellowship to those joined in common concerns and responsibilities. We could see no possibility of establishing real fellowship, with the significance which Methodists have traditionally given to it, or as Gordon Strutt had pictured it, apart from a minor revolution in our accepted routine and priorities. Neville concluded that the eight House Churches should be prepared to break in half to provide the nucleus of sixteen Anglican-Methodist groups. Ernest was convinced that what we had in mind was impracticable apart from an explicit commitment on the part of the engaging churches to make the fellowship group the agreed priority for the whole adult church during the first seven days of each calendar month. In the autumn of 1963 both the Parochial Church Council and the two Leaders' Meetings gave formal approval to the two suggestions: the Anglicans would divide their House Churches; the Methodists would abandon their week-night Guild or Church Fellowship during the first seven days of the month. 'Home Fellowship' became the accepted title and the 'explosion' of the Church into the home was timed for January 1964.

Resolutions were followed by much practical preparation. At St. Mary Magdalene and the two Methodist Churches special notice boards were erected for the exclusive use of the Home Fellowship organisation. The notice boards were divided into seven sections, one for each day of the week, and provided for the pinning-up of special post-cards announcing details of the group meetings. Over the years we have not found it necessary to alter the general form of the cards. They were headed 'Addiscombe Churches' (now 'The Addiscombe Group of Churches') and read: '*Home Fellowships*. You are invited to join the group which is to meet in the home of . . . at 8.00 p.m. on . . . day . . . Subject: . . . Group Number . . .' On the right-hand side of the card we reserved a space for

'Those hoping to attend from this Church'—an encouragement to persons looking for someone to accompany them. Since it was envisaged that groups should be mobile—moving from home to home—and open—ready to accept the newcomer, the notice boards and Group Numbers were almost indispensable. They made it possible for Ministers to plan pastoral visits and provided a ready-reference for enquirers. At the same time, the more important work was going ahead, finding homes, securing the intial leadership and making lists of the potential group members. Homes were in abundant supply. From hosts we asked for help in the invitation of neighbours, but beyond this, requested no more than the provision of a room and the simplest of refreshments. For evident reasons, the refreshment-rule was of the utmost importance: fellowship could be destroyed by over-lavish hospitality. Leadership-commitment, in the first place, was limited to the conduct of an initial, exploratory gathering, but it was hoped that groups would wish to meet on a regular basis and most of our leaders were willing to contemplate an on-going group life. 'Guests' were invited to 'meet some of our Anglican/Methodist neighbours' but the understanding was that we looked forward to meeting fellow-Christians of all persuasions. Looking back, we are somewhat amazed that so many were willing to commit themselves to the largely unknown experience of inter-church lay fellowship. Some leaders might have reason to claim that they were 'thrown into it' with very little training or guidance from their ministers. Yet the post-cards began to appear on the boards: Wednesday overflowed (Saturday was the only blank), and during the first seven days of January 1964 we held our twenty-four 'House-Warmings'.

Hosts and leaders had already received our suggestions for the conduct of the 'House-Warming'. We suggested a simple pattern of devotion and a period of personal introductions followed by discussion of possible courses of study. Groups contemplating future meetings were asked to make the fullest possible use of the invitation cards, completing them for church notice-boards, for the appropriate clergy and for neighbours who could not be contacted in a more personal way. All the groups agreed to continue, at least for a period, the majority choosing to study the *Conversations*; three groups chose an appropriate Bible study theme, assisted by Frederick Greeves in 'God's Fellow-Workers'; one began the study of Mark's Gospel, and another created its own syllabus by inviting members of the group (of four denominations) to speak in turn about their own church. As the two ministers responsible for the fellowships, we had hoped that it might be possible for one or the other of us to visit each group quarterly. If we succeeded in the first few months it was for the first and last time. In practice we found it impossible to keep in as close touch as we believed (and as experience has taught us) we should. In May 1964 we resorted to the first of our joint 'epistles'. We conveyed our greetings and rejoiced in what we had seen and heard. We left to the groups the decision about their summer recess, raised the matter of future study material and asked that action be taken to reach out beyond the Anglican-Methodist boundaries. The particular concern of this first letter was that all groups should come together on a Sunday evening in July to learn of each other's doings and to plan for the future. At the evening service preceding the United Home Fellowship gathering, we exchanged pulpits, Ernest preaching at St. Mary Magdalene and Neville conducting worship and administering the Holy Communion at the Addiscombe Methodist Church.

The united gathering, once or twice in the year, has become an essential feature of the group life; the first had a quality of its own: perhaps it lay in the sense of discovery. It appeared that five groups had lost their separate existence, one by immediately sub-dividing (we have tried to make it a rule that groups should not be larger than twelve), four by linking with other groups. Twenty active groups remained. Requests were made by largely Methodist groups for an infusion of Anglicans, from largely Anglican groups for Methodists. Such pleas have become familiar and have not been easily met. At the same time we found that more than half the groups had already brought in members of other denominations and were planning to move on from the *Conversations* to Bible Study or wider concerns. Above all, the group reports witnessed to the rich experience of learning *together*, of seeing something that had not been seen before and of that joy in each other's company which faith interprets as the work of the Holy Spirit. It was from this point of discovery that in the autumn of 1964 we wrote to the groups again, sharing our thoughts about future developments. One matter concerned courtesy towards local Anglican incumbents. 'Our' groups were meeting in as many as six parishes, and while their membership was drawn in the first place from our own congregations, neighbour was inviting neighbour and the membership of other churches than our own was becoming involved. We therefore asked groups to extend to their local Anglican minister (and to ministers of other churches known to be working in their area) the courtesy of a monthly post-card, and when possible, an invitation to speak to the group. These suggestions were taken up by some, but the impression of 'invasion' or 'empire-building' has faded away only as the colleagueship of two has found its place within a wider group ministry.

It was in 1964 that we tried to give further help to the Home Fellowships by providing an 'Outline Agenda'. There seemed little response at the time, but later this kind of guidance has proved more welcome. The idea was drawn in part from an 'Agenda for Class Meetings' produced by the Church Membership Committee of the Methodist Church and in part from the method of Bible Study associated with the name of Johannes Hamel.

AGENDA FOR HOME FELLOWSHIPS

Opening Devotions. Silence. Short prayer.

1. THE BIBLE

Reading of selected passage, preferably from several versions.

Results of prepared study of passage presented by member deputed last time.

Questions and discussion aimed at uncovering the full meaning of the passage.

Summary of findings by member responsible for the preparation. (20 minutes)

2. THE WORLD

What service did we undertake at the last meeting? Have we done it?

Are there any special concerns which members wish to share with the group? (A member previously deputed may here present, as factually as possible, some practical concern.)

Questions and discussion aimed at uncovering relevant aspects of the subject.

Summary of findings by member made responsible. (20 minutes)

3. THE CHURCH

How does the Bible passage bear upon the concerns we have examined?

What action are we led to take?

Has anyone sought our prayers? Does anyone need our prayers?

(Prayer time, including silent intercession may follow.)

Who among us will lead *a.* Bible Study, *b.* the Concern, *c.* the prayers, when we next meet? Where and when do we meet next? Who will undertake the *immediate* preparation of the Home Fellowship invitation cards *a.* for churches, *b.* for ministers, *c.* for individuals?

Who should receive a personal invitation to the next meeting? Closing devotions. Silence. Intercessory prayer. Prayer of committal, with or without the Lord's Prayer. The Grace, said together. (20 minutes)

Refreshments may suitably be introduced between 2 and 3 or after closing devotions. Discipline of time and subject matter is more likely to be of use to the Holy Spirit than an indefinite free-for-all. All questions under 3 should be found place *without fail* at each meeting.

In preparation for the united Home Fellowships gathering in July 1965, we asked groups to complete a questionnaire to replace extensive verbal reports. These were loyally completed and gave a ready picture of the situation: continually changing with movement of population and alteration in domestic circumstances, but revealing nearly twenty groups with a distinctive and developing life. Bible Study had been the main subject matter with different groups studying Mark, Acts, Romans, 1 Corinthians and Revelation. Four groups had worked on questions and Bible references based on the five sections of the Nottingham Conference—the First British Conference on Faith and Order held at Nottingham in September 1964. Ministers of various denominations, including Roman Catholic and Baptist, had been the guests of several groups. One complaint was that the Anglican 'No Small Change' study course was creating a conflict of loyalty and that one church had broken the 'seven-day' rule. A more serious complaint was that the Ministers were pressing for the sub-division of groups too quickly and failing to recognise the desire of members to remain identified with a particular fellowship. A small but significant matter affected a proposed new group which would meet on the edge of our recognised geographical area; after consultation we passed the responsibility for its development and oversight to a Congregational Minister within the neighbouring South Norwood Group of Churches.

Written reports made it possible for the 1965 United Gathering to give time to two special 'concerns': these related to the intercessory and healing work of the Church. One group, with a total membership of fifteen, including Anglicans, Methodists, Roman Catholics, one Dutch Reformed and one Salvation Army, had recently been formed under the inspiration of 'S.C.K.'—the Servants of Christ the King.[2] Some of the emphases of this movement were soon to become widely known through the 'People Next Door' programme. These include the conception of the group as an organic whole (not a miniature audience), leadership as not dependent on any one individual, and the importance of each member to the common life. Success in this type of group is seen in the ability of each to accept the other, to listen sensitively and without condemnation, to bear the expression of personal feelings and to spend time in unhurried, silent intercession.[3] Ministerially, we viewed this development with some caution, fearing the introspective piety which we associated, from our second-hand knowledge, with the inter-war 'Oxford Group' movement and features of a much earlier form of Methodism. An exposition of the aims of the S.C.K. movement within a parochial context helped us to see it in clearer perspective, and we have since had reason to be grateful to this group as one to which we knew we could turn to give support to a person with a history of several years of drug addiction.

Fears, frequently expressed, that the Home Fellowship is open to the dangers of sectarianism and heresy, have not, in our experience, been fully allayed. The dangers were in our minds when we substituted 'Home Fellowship' for 'House Church'. For two years one of our groups laboured under an assertive Pentecostalism. The almost continuous assault on the

[2] Founded by Canon Roger Lloyd of Westminster. See Appendix 'Addresses'.

[3] See *Dynamics of the Small Group*, Clinical Theory pamphlet no. 2. Also *Practical Notes on Conducting a Session of Waiting upon God*, S.C.K.

faith and practice of other members was the more saddening since the group had set itself to listen with sympathy to the claims of the Pentecostal movement and was composed of some of our most mature members. Concern rose to crisis when Father McKenna, our Roman Catholic colleague, visiting a Home Fellowship for the first time, found that there was little room for him to make any contribution. We have always felt a debt of gratitude to him that this experience was not allowed to affect his relationship with us or the presence of some of his own people in the groups. We also reflect on the quality of Christian charity exhibited by the group members. Their affection and respect for the person concerned remained throughout the difficult period, and in another group he was able to contribute his gifts much more helpfully. Three members of this group had a deep sense of call to provide a 'halfway' home for drug addicts, patients newly recovering after treatment in mental hospital, and others in similar need. Impossible as their project seemed at first, they are now responsible for such a home in the locality, largely through the cooperation of the Woodside Baptist Church.

A second group was assailed by the 'prophetic' theories of a Bible student with several publications to his name. Finding herself in the presence of a man of considerable learning, the appointed leader quietly had to retire into the background. The new leader's loyal avoidance of British Israelite teaching, his careful preparation and the respect in which he was held by us all, made it difficult to know what action to take. A ministerial visit led to a clash over the definition of 'prophecy' and seemed unfruitful. Meanwhile we felt that the members of the group were being subjected to a subtle 'gnosticism' which exalted private biblical theories over biblical faith, and we knew that some of the teaching was anti-Roman Catholic and implicitly anti-clerical. We made enquiries from members in our pastoral care but otherwise took no action. Eventually, common sense and loyalty to their own ministers led to three of our members leaving and the group ceased to have *formal* association with the Addiscombe Group of Churches.

As we prepared for the United Home Fellowship Gathering of July 1966, 'Group Dynamics' and 'P.N.D. 1967' appear to have been of more immediate concern to us than minor outbreaks of unorthodoxy. As a variation on the Report-back, we dared to set 'Summer (self-) Examinations'. Readers may find the question-paper of interest:

Qualification required: Honesty. All questions to be attempted.

1. What has the Home Fellowship meant to each member? You have become familiar with the views of each other; what have you learned of Christ?

2. Is it possible that the pleasure derived by some has been at the expense of others? Have any members felt 'out' of the group? Who have ceased to come and why?

3. What impression would your group give to a new-comer who was *a*. Church-going, *b*. Non-church-going? Is your group flexible and sensitive enough to 'take in' new members?

4. Have you learned to be open with each other? Do you ever dare to be angry? Are you aware of barriers, pretences or evasions?

5. Groups are sometimes described as either 'person-centred' or 'work-centred'. How would you describe your group?

6. How do you envisage the future development of your group? Do you think your group is playing its full part in the life of its members, the Church and the community?

7. Are you willing to face the prospect of your group subdividing to form the nucleus of a new one? If you resist this prospect, why?

8. What assistance do you feel most in need of?

9. Which of these questions have you most resented, and why?

10. What marks do you allocate yourselves on the above examination:

    a. for honesty? *b.* for charity? *c.* for vision?

Question 10 was the most resented. Most groups gave themselves 100% passes.

The 'S.C.K.-type' group provided an answer to question 1 which summarises, what, at their best, the Home Fellowships have meant: 'The group feels that it is really beginning to thaw out now. We have learnt that we are indeed interdependent . . . how much we affect each other. We have learnt, too, how little we know, and how much we need to learn and desire to learn, especially in deeper knowledge and understanding of the Bible. We have all had to make more effort. We have all read more books. We have all found the group a stimulus and have found greater understanding of what we believe. We have learnt to pray together and have found a new dimension in group prayer. We have learnt to be silent together . . . some of us find this living silence a great help, and it has played a big part . . . in our learning of Christ. (An intercessory fellowship has grown out of the group, and this uses the silence, the waiting upon God, for longer periods.) One member says she has learnt to pray for the first time. We have a true sense of fellowship and truly feel part of the Body of Christ, not only when we meet in the group, but . . . also when we cannot attend meetings . . .'

Looking back over the first four years of the Home Fellowship movement in Addiscombe, we begin to understand why the 'People Next Door'[4] course for study and action, planned to take place during Lent 1967, failed to make an impression upon our people comparable with that reported from other areas. Our initial objective, to double the number of Fellowships, was misjudged and probably unwise. The position began

---

[4] See Appendices, p. 163, "P.N.D".

to emerge in the autumn of 1966, when attendance at the Leadership Training Course revealed that few new leaders would be forthcoming. Existing leaders were 'at full stretch' and others capable of leadership were involved in the Church's pastoral out-reach described in the next chapter. Having faced a barrage of courses and enquiries for 36 months, from the *Conversations*, Nottingham, our own 'Croydon Nottingham', the Croydon Council of Churches, 'No Small Change'[5] and, not least, from us, the ministers, our people were in no mood to believe that another course, however well conceived, could have anything really new to say. The suggestion of 'stepping-up' meetings from monthly to fortnightly, to make possible the completion of P.N.D. during the first three months of the year, did not help to relieve the anxiety. Nevertheless, during the first half of 1967 fourteen groups, out of a new total of twenty-four, made use of the P.N.D. material, four of these meetings as Lenten groups only. The challenge to learn more of our neighbours, both within and without the Church, resulted in the formation of two quite new groups, including our first truly multi-racial fellowship. Three groups of neighbours were left waiting for a leader to get them 'off the mark'. Muslims and Mormons were among guest speakers and one of us shared an evening with professed agnostics.

Two features of the 'People Next Door' phase seemed particularly significant. First, it marked the transition from an ecumenical work deriving principally from our own colleague-ship (and the special relationship of St. Mary Magdalene and Addiscombe Methodist) to a work under the direction of an inter-church ministerial staff. In this ministerial oversight we were able to enlist the help of a lay organiser and liaison officer. The circular letter of March 1967 was the last to go out over our two signatures. Of particular satisfaction to the Addiscombe

---

[5] A course of lay training prepared for use in the Church of England during Lent 1965.

Methodist Church was the sense of re-establishing a full working-relationship with St. Mildred's, the Anglican community with which it had made its first adventures in fellowship. The second feature was the spontaneous request of groups for a practical objective of service to the community. Reports desired 'a proper aim', 'some other contacts', 'local ecumenical neighbourhood projects', 'prayer-supported action', 'courses less theoretical'. A long-standing group member, whose responsibilities included: 1. the maintenance of an effective Christian Aid Week organisation in the parish, 2. the development of the two-year-old inter-church Community Centre, 3. a 'stint' of door-to-door visiting, 4. the pastoral care of a Methodist 'Class', and 5. his commitments as a member of the Samaritans (for the befriending of those tempted to despair or suicide) lost no time in providing groups with what they had asked for. A letter was circulating almost (but not quite) before it had received the ministerial blessing.

'One of the most significant contributions to the renewal of the Church in each place.'[6] We would assent to this judgement of the Home Fellowship, as we have seen it and as we have, inadequately, sought to foster it. Within the total life of the Church (not outside it), the fellowships have been the places of discovery: discovery of one another and discovery of the unfolding purposes for which God has bound us together. The discovery of one another was possible only in the daunting intimacy of personal encounter; the discovery of our joint mission was only possible within the new context of mutual acceptance and recognition. We look back now with astonishment to think there should ever have been a time when three family groups could issue forth from the same road Sunday after Sunday to make their way to their accustomed places of worship, and do this year after year without even knowing each other's names or the barest acknowledgement that they

[6] *British Council of Churches 'Work-book' 2*, page 11.

were about the same business. We are appalled to think that, each in his own church has 'prayed' and 'given' for the work of 'Mission' while the mission-field of the street waited for its Christians to recognise each other's existence. The over-riding result of the Home Fellowship has been the discovery of the Church in the Road. To this discovery the 'Home Mission' or House Visiting, has made its own indispensable contribution: to this we now turn.

4. In the Road

THE work described in this chapter has to be understood in relation to the social background previously described[1]—a high-density population with a ten per cent annual change-over. But our work in much smaller urban units suggests that our experience is not irrelevant wherever a high proportion of the population is personally unknown to the Church except as names on an electoral register. To this unknown pastorate, our churches, four years ago, were giving a measure of recognition. The Parish Church had a very long-established distribution network which placed 3,200 'Addiscombe Reviews' free in each home in the Parish, every month. A network of standardised notice-boards, approximately one in every road, supplemented the magazine distribution by high-lighting special events. A card-index system had been built up covering every home. The Methodists distributed their News-letter widely on a selective basis and circularised five and a half thousand homes in their immediate catchment area two or three times a year. With the development of joint activity it was felt needful to make a gesture of our intention to the neighbourhood and on a Sunday afternoon in October 1964 about six hundred people, of all ages and including West Indians, processed around the Parish under four banners bearing the legend 'The Church in Addiscombe'.

In unobtrusive ways, many of our people were already active, outside the bounds of any formal church association, in the service of their neighbours. But it was evident that the overwhelming proportion of people living around our churches was untouched in any personal way by the Church in their

[1] Chapter 2.

midst. Concern was expressed at the Parochial Church Council Retreat in 1961, when prominence was given to the Oval Road section of the Parish. House to house visiting by the assistant curates had shown 'that we are out of touch with many people'. It was felt that training would be necessary before lay visiting in cooperation with the Methodists could be contemplated. The impression given by the reports is that the P.C.C. was still relying primarily on the paid church worker to keep open the lines of communication. Three years passed before the issue of joint lay visitation was raised again; this time it came from a fifty-strong Pastoral Committee, which met in July 1964. Present were Methodist Class Leaders, Anglican Church Visitors, and representatives of the West Indian 'Church of God' meeting at the Cherry Orchard Methodist Church premises. The following recommendations were approved for submission to the respective churches, which in due course gave their approval:

1. That the Parish Church of St. Mary Magdalene, the Methodist Churches of Addiscombe and Cherry Orchard, the Church of God, West Indies, and other churches at work in the area, roughly between Windmill Bridge and Bingham Station, forthwith join forces in a regular and continuing ministry of door to door visitation.

2. That the Mission be known as 'The Church In Addiscombe Home Mission'.

3. That Mission head-quarters be established for the time being at the Methodist premises, 114 Lower Addiscombe Road.

4. That the head-quarters provide the necessary office accommodation and facilities including:

a. Wall-map of District, with streets, wards and parishes clearly marked and signs to indicate where visiting is in progress.

b. Card Index covering all homes and collating the records of the partner churches.

c. Visitation record forms and other basic material for use of visitors.

5. That this mission be understood to involve each and every member of our congregations, according to their strength and ability; that each member accept responsibility, when requested to pray for a neighbour or to offer friendship; that through the maps and by other means the Mission be kept before the minds of our people; that the advance work be committed to persons willing to commit themselves to regular visiting on a weekly, fortnightly or monthly basis; that the advance work be consolidated by persons willing to exercise a continuing pastoral ministry to all 'contacts'; that Tuesday be at present the main Mission night, though other nights and times will be used by those for whom Tuesday is not convenient; that visitation be normally two by two, preferably by people representing two different churches; that devotions precede each visitation; that starting-time be as soon after 7.30 p.m. as possible.

6. That the ministers act as the organising committee, with power to co-opt lay helpers as they deem fit; that lay secretaries be found to help in analysing information and passing it to the appropriate quarters, maintaining maps and records . . . that the Ministers be responsible for preparing the joint literature and the Tuesday night training and prayer sessions; that a special Service of Dedication be held in St. Mary Magdalene on Saturday, 12 September and that the first evening of Training and Visiting be held in the Addiscombe Methodist Church on Tuesday, 13 October. (Some already had experience of the visiting work and were willing to go out in the knowledge that others were engaged in prayer and preparation.)

The 'Service of Dedication for Home Mission' was held as planned. The day was not well chosen, though it seemed the only suitable occasion at the time. About sixty persons were present, some 'on the understanding' that they were willing to pray for the work of Home Mission but not necessarily to take an active part. The Service began with silent and spoken prayer, followed by the hymn to the Holy Spirit, 'Lord God, the Holy Ghost'. The Bible reading was of the mission of the Seventy and the address was given by our Baptist colleague, the Rev. Leslie Moxham, who spoke on the 'house to house' ministry recalled by the Apostle Paul in his farewell to the elders of Miletus. We invited extempore contributions to the second period of prayer and invited the congregation to share in words from the Methodist Covenant Service as the Act of Commitment. We used the following bidding to lead to the final Act:

'LET US REMEMBER how Jesus said, the harvest is plenteous but the labourers are few; pray ye therefore the Lord of the harvest that he send forth labourers into his harvest . . .

how Jesus sent his disciples two by two before his face into every city whither he himself was about to come . . .

how Jesus said, I came not to call the righteous, but sinners . . .

how men said of him that he was the sinners' friend.

LET US PRAY that the Holy Spirit will teach us the meaning of these words . . .

that we may share our Lord's compassion for the multitudes . . .

that we may be given the wisdom which knows that ploughing and sowing must come before harvest . . .

that we may have the humility to accept that it is not given to all men to harvest what they have sown . . .

that our sense of inadequacy may itself be an instrument in the Master's hands . . .

that we may go to people with the right word on our lips and in our hearts . . .

that having learnt all we are able of the message we bring and of the work we have to do, we may trust in the guidance of the Holy Spirit in every situation . . .

that we may not grow weary in well doing . . .

that as we prepare the way for Christ, we may know that he also prepares the way for us . . .
that we may never doubt Christ's love for any man, nor his power to save, nor that in any man which can respond to the love of God in Christ . . .
LET US THEN as many as are willing by God's Grace, commit ourselves to God and to all that he wills for us, saying together . . . I am no longer my own but thine. Put me to what thou wilt . . .'

When we held our 'Service of Renewal' for the Door to Door Visiting team at St. Luke's in April 1968, the following Act of Dedication was substituted for the words of Covenant:

> O Lord, who sent your disciples in
> twos ahead of you to every place you
> were going to visit,
> Send us where you wish us to go,
> Tell us what you wish us to speak,
> Encourage us, whether people refuse us
>   or listen;
> And to you, not to us, be the glory
> throughout time and for ever.   Amen

Careful preparation was made for the first evening of visiting and training. The only type of filing cabinet available to us dictated a visitors' report-form duplicated on foolscap. This we have not had reason to change. It reads, in essentials:

STREET OR ROAD

NUMBERS . . . TO . . .

NUMBER/NAME *a. b. c.* SURNAME TITLE AFFILIATION/INTERESTS

a. Visit paid. *b.* Interest-finder or other literature supplied. *c.* Interview.

We duplicated a second type of form, for the use of visitors wishing to pass on information immediately to clergy or lay leaders: this was confined to the information that 'the above is interested in . . .' and 'a suitable time for a visit is . . .' A third form was prepared as an 'Interest Finder' summarising the activities of the local churches and providing the names and addresses of all ministers and clergy. Space was provided for the ticking of items of interest and the entering of name and address; enquirers could then send the form to the Minister of their choice. These three forms, clipped to twelve cut-out boards, provided the basic equipment of the visitor. We also prepared pochettes, containing such items as Church magazines, syllabuses and details of other voluntary organisations, for instance, the Darby and Joan Club and Toc H. These 'tools for the job' were laid out in the room which the Methodists made available and outside, in the foyer, a twenty-four inch map of the area was displayed on its own permanent notice board. The map, carefully prepared by a helper, showed the boundaries of the Anglican parishes, together with the smaller areas—corresponding to polling wards—into which we had divided the parishes for the more effective organisation of the Home fellowships and the pastoral care. We arranged for the premises to be open to visitors on every night of the week.

October 13th came, and only about a dozen workers reported for duty. The Home Mission thereon failed to gather momentum and by Christmas it was non-operational. The failure appears to have been on the two levels of communication and organisation. We failed to communicate our intention to provide specific training and found that some, already committed on Tuesdays, supposed that they were precluded from participating. Our most serious mistake was to suppose that 'operational' visitors would be willing to turn up any night at the Home Mission centre, look for a partner, examine the records and then without further advice or encouragement, say their prayers and take up the work where a predecessor had left off. Twelve dwindled to two and then to nil. In the general uncertainty two visitors came along one night to find that even the minister was not on duty at the agreed place at the right time. An endeavour begun with all seriousness had petered out.

The Home Mission came to life again the following year through the concern of some of our laymen and the encouragement of our Roman Catholic colleagues. In April 1965 a 'men's committee' was gathered together at the Addiscombe Roman Catholic Church for the purpose of examining the task of house-to-house visiting. The representation was greatly extended and included, for the first time, the neighbouring Anglican parishes of St. Mildred's and St. Luke's together with our host church. It was decided to promote a 'pilot' scheme of visiting in a road of about two hundred houses lying roughly central to our joint area. Twenty-four men, eight from each of the three denominations involved, were called to a briefing meeting in June and the visiting took place in July. Significant features of the new work were the inter-parish basis, the guidance and support of other ministerial colleagues and above all, the allocation of a specific group of houses to each pair of visitors and the defining of a time and place for the Report-back. So emerged a pattern of work which has now become normal to the life of the churches in Addiscombe. Though a heavy responsibility of follow-up work fell to several ministers, it was felt right to proceed with a second 'stint' of visiting, this time in a post-war housing area, and this was carried out in October.

The Home Mission, as it has developed, will best be described by our lay Organiser; but it may be appropriate, first, to comment on the twin question of 'objects' and 'results'. The former question was on several occasions put to us by the Baptist observer on our local Council of Churches (later 'Group Council'). Our understanding, from the beginning, was that the object was to 'commend Christ'. This commending of Christ, as we saw it in relation to our neighbours, involved the preparedness to meet people on their own ground, to meet them in humility and to meet them in the conciousness of their unique value to God. We were not able to equate this approach with ecclesiastical canvassing, whether for a particular 'church' or dogma. We believed our initial task, as far as possible was to listen rather than to accost, address or even question. If at a few doors some small confidence could be won, some want expressed, some need half-voiced, some avenue of understanding found, the journey was not in vain. We never found it possible to define the objects to the complete satisfaction of all those dedicated to them. Some at first felt the need to justify the visiting by specifying a particular object—perhaps the discovery of the house-bound and lonely—others asked whether our objects should be a 'survey' of human need, complete with consultant sociologist and questionnaire. But as the months have passed and experience has been shared it is noticeable that the work has provided its own authentication and satisfied the visitors that it does not need any obvious justification. No longer is it felt needful to define precise limits within which the visitors may work: the understanding is that they may take their interview as far as they are jointly led to believe they may go. The point is partly illustrated by the change we have made in the wording of the introductory leaflet. In July and October 1965 it read as follows.

HOME MISSION

Representatives of the Anglican, Methodist and Roman Catholic Churches in the Addiscombe District will be calling on you in the course of the next two weeks. The churches are concerned to know in what ways they may be able to help you, and in particular to learn from you about any housebound invalid or lonely people.

Yours sincerely,
The Clergy and Ministers of the Addiscombe area

A year later (the district concerned was one for which no Roman Catholic visitors were available) the offer of 'help' had been discreetly dropped. We were content to say:

Two visitors representing the Church of England, Methodist and other churches will be calling on you in the near future. They would appreciate a little of your time and will be grateful to know of any family or neighbourhood needs.

The practical results of a ministry of 'front-line' visiting are an ever increasing burden of pastoral responsibility. The burden would be intolerable apart from the conviction which brought us to it and the fact of the churches bearing it together. Where visitors are able to report a specific request—a visit from Minister or Priest, an introduction to Wives' Club, Community Centre, Youth Club or Sunday School—'follow-up' is reasonably straightforward; but in the majority of cases where interest is shown our course of action is less clearly defined. Visitors may guess at unspoken needs and suggest that a further visit, ministerial or lay, might be appreciated; sometimes it appears that more information should be obtained, and in this case there might be consultation with the Welfare authorities. At all events, the aim is to entrust the particular responsibility to the person or the body appropriate to the need. It may be to one of the clergy, a lay organiser or road warden, it may be to a Home Fellowship, some voluntary association, or a statutory body. Report-back meetings have revealed greatly divergent responses made to different pairs of visitors, some finding a 'welcome' in almost every home, others an almost universal lack of interest. These discoveries have led us to an honest assessment of our personal gifts and limitations and to 'repairing' where a more effective partnership may be created. Yet even the most 'successful' visitors go out on their work in the knowledge that 'calculable' response is not likely in more than a fraction of the homes visited. Here is probably the biggest challenge to the intention and integrity of the workers; to believe that the visit is not in vain where the report may still read 'not interested', that God has means of communication not discernible on the door-step.

In March 1966 Miss Dorothy Cornwall took over the Home Mission organisation from Ernest Goodridge and gave up her retirement to the full time service of the church. Her work quickly made her, in effect, a lay member of an inter-church team ministry. Her work will be seen to exceed what we had envisaged in our original proposals and it has been directly responsible for the transformation of an informal ministers' fraternal into a joint ministerial staff meeting. Miss Cornwall describes the work and development of the Home Mission and as its voluntary organiser.

'At the meeting of the ministerial staff I am instructed to make arrangements for a certain road or district to be visited. At this point I may be compelled to ask for more visitors, or mention that the visitors from one of the churches have dropped off. My remarks are always noted. The staff have never yet failed to find the visitors needed. Indeed, this kind of door-to-door visiting, though it requires courage, actually attracts some church members. At the beginning all were men but some women are now included.

'My first step is to telephone the forty-odd visitors on my list, to ask them if they can take part in the visitation of . . . Road during the following weeks. If they are not on the telephone I go round to see them. By some means I get their response and usually find that there are about twenty who can do it. These have to be arranged in pairs and my instructions are to link them as far as possible with someone of another denomination. There are exceptions, such as a husband and wife who want to work together, and sometimes the denominations are not evenly represented. I plan it the best way I can. Next I make a preliminary survey of the road, walking along both sides and seeing the exact number of visits to be made.

Large apartment houses, with seven or eight bells on the front door, are probably the most difficult task the visitors have to face. Three or four of these would be equal to twenty small houses. By the number of visitors available and the number of houses I have to decide whether the road can be completed in one visitation. A long main road, for example, might be divided into three sections and become the subject of three visitations.

'Report sheets are prepared for the visitors. Four houses per foolscap sheet work out well, special provision being made, of course, for exceptional cases like the apartment houses. An introductory leaflet is typed and duplicated. The visitors are asked to drop this in the letter boxes a few days before they call. There is another typed leaflet, an interest-finder, which describes the opportunities for worship and service offered by the churches as a whole both to children and adults. This is distributed by the visitors wherever they think it is appropriate. At length I write to the visitors who have consented to do the assignment, telling them who is their partner, the date of the report-back meeting and any news of interest. To one of each pair I send the allocation of report sheets and a supply of leaflets. Their task usually works out at sixteen to twenty visits.

'The routine so far described refers to visiting in an established area. Where new developments are concerned the approach is a little different. We have had to deal with one such housing development by the London Borough of Croydon, consisting of four blocks of flats, eleven storeys each and totalling 175 units. Eighty-six of these flats were designated "Sheltered Housing for Elderly People". As each flat became occupied, a welcoming note from the Group of Churches was delivered. It informed tenants about the nearest churches and the times of Sunday Worship and Sunday Schools. It invited them to ask for information and gave my name and address as Group Organiser. After giving them a few weeks to settle in, the visitors delivered their introductory leaflet, indicating that they would be calling and that they would be able to give any information wanted about church or welfare activities. When they made their call they had with them lists of facilities available in the district with names and addresses of persons who could be contacted. The visitors reported a good reception and progress was slow because they were often invited in. In these particular flats there were known to be a great number of elderly women living alone; there were also some intermittent church-goers who had been moved by our welcoming note to consider whether in a new district they might make a new start and perhaps through a church find new friends. On the whole it was a favourable field for the visitors and for the ministerial staff when they followed up. No one doubted the wisdom of being there right at the start.

'To return to the organisation's general practice, it is clearly understood by all visitors that they represent not their own church but all the churches in the group. This is a factor which surprises many of the people they interview. Approval is frequently expressed, if only in the words "and about time too".

'The date and place of the meeting to which the visitors will bring back their reports is fixed for four to six weeks ahead, giving them plenty of time for repeated visits to people who are out. After three unsuccessful visits they leave a visiting card, inviting the occupier to ask for information. It is very important that at least one of the Ministerial Staff should be present to meet the visitors when they report back and this too is arranged. The report-back meeting is a friendly one, at which visitors meet one another, hand in their written reports and give a brief account of their experiences. They have the opportunity of making suggestions, asking questions and seeking guidance.

'In the next few days I extract from the reports those which relate to people expressing interest in particular churches and despatch copies to the appropriate Vicar, Minister or Priest.

This applies to ALL churches in the Group, including four not represented on the Ministerial Staff, and also to neighbouring churches outside the area of the group. Reports which say "No answer" or "No interest" are for the time being disregarded, but it is hoped that in later visiting the response may be found to be different. The remaining reports relate to people who talked to the visitors but did not mention any church affiliation. These reports are also listed and submitted to the Ministerial Staff at their next meeting for allocation as they think best. For the sake of quick action it is clear that a meeting of the staff must follow closely after the report-back meeting of the visitors. The time sequence of events is important in the planning of the whole of this programme, from the Ministerial Staff Meeting at which it is instigated to the meeting at which the information gets back to the staff. At present my official records show only the church or voluntary body to which each of the visitors' reports has been commended. A system is envisaged by which a note of the action taken will eventually be passed back to me for the records. The principle has been accepted that a records office, situated for practical convenience in each Anglican Parish, shall house all records and be open to all churches. The Addiscombe Methodist Church provided the centre for the Parish of St. Mary Magdalene.

'A second line of visitors has had to be found to help the clergy in the follow-up work. These helpers are willing, circumstances allowing, to sit with the house-bound, do shopping or other essential errands, talk about domestic problems, comfort, sympathise, or just listen. They are not Welfare Officers and do not attempt to do the work which should be done by experts. They offer friendship and try to demonstrate that they really care.

'The setting up of this second line of helpers was the greatest difficulty we have encountered so far. It had to depend, initially, on the systems of church visitors and road wardens already existing in some of the churches. The task had to be attempted to re-organise these on an area basis and to bring in visitors from churches which formerly had none. We had to encourage visitors from various churches to work more closely together. The results were not immediately satisfactory, but the helpers available have always just managed to accomplish the work. The first-line visiting has sometimes discovered new helpers. It was not until a remarkable gathering of about eighty Road Wardens and Church Visitors in February 1968 and the larger gathering of workers the following month at the Addiscombe/ Shirley Study Conference on "Christian Care and the Welfare Services" that the uncertainties seemed to disappear and the "second-line" work "came alight".

'It is admitted that these helpers have the most exacting task in the organisation. Anyone who does it must have time, compassion, patience, understanding and forbearance; she (or he) must be prepared to listen and never be provoked; she may have to go on with it for a long time. Unlike the professional, who visits, keeps detached, advises and then goes away again, the church visitor, whose neighbours may be physically above, around and beneath her, has to stay with it and become involved. Only by entering into the other person's problem can she really help, and this is specially demanding when the other person through illness or long habit, does not cooperate. In the latter case the helper is likely to fail, or at best suffer from fatigue, unless she knows how to become the instrument of a greater care than her own. In other words, this is work for Christians, for people who will go the extra mile.

'It is not always hard. There have been many cases where a real and delightful friendship has been established. When it does become hard, there are ways of lightening the burden. Experiment has shown that demanding circumstances are best shared by two visitors or even three. The House Groups meeting all over the area are being drawn into the organisation and they are sometimes asked to take a practical interest in someone who needs a friend.

'The professional workers have recognised the value of the organisation. The Welfare Officer may be able to call once a month, but only someone who lives near can keep watch or make the frequent visits that some elderly or handicapped people need. The Old People's Welfare Department and the Moral Welfare Association have both used the church organisation. They give me information over the telephone about cases where they think that friendship can help, and from my list I select someone living in the same area and discover if she is free to go. If all the visitors are fully occupied I refer the case to the nearest member of the Ministerial Staff and ask him to find a visitor. One has always been found.

'The most recent development has come from a local mental hospital and illustrates the way in which this kind of service ignores denominational barriers. The hospital, on discharging certain patients, has commended them to the care of the Croydon Deanery. The Deanery Social Worker has then made use of the church organisation in Addiscombe. For example a woman discharged from the hospital was a Roman Catholic. She was being advised by the Anglican Deanery Social Worker and encouraged to go to weekly social gatherings at the nearby Methodist Church in the care of a friendly Methodist. This experiment was watched by the mental hospital doctors. It is impossible to escape the challenging conclusion that the churches are being placed on trial. As we go forward, I confess to feeling some excitement and a great deal of awe.

'In 1967 the Addiscombe Group of Churches decided to adopt the *Ichthus* (the ancient sign of the fish) together with the *Chi-Rho* device, as a kind of trade-mark for the united operations of the churches. It was carefully designed by one of the staff in red and black and now appears strikingly on the leaflets used by visitors, on visiting cards and on correspondence paper.

It has appeared in Parish Magazines. Printed on a 6" × 12" card, the sign is displayed by "Church Contacts" (usually Road Wardens) in their front windows. The display of the sign indicates that here lives someone connected with one of the local churches and willing to provide information to enquirers. Church contacts possess files, or have a file available nearby containing information about all church activities, welfare facilities and social clubs in the immediate neighbourhood. Gathering the information and distributing it had been a tremendous task and it will need amendments from time to time. At Whitsun 1967 the cards began to appear throughout the area, arousing, as was hoped, both curiosity and enquiry. Addiscombe has become aware of this silent witness, what it means and what it offers. It is expected that more church members will be encouraged to display the sign as time goes on; it is already having the desirable effect of making the members of different churches known to one another.

'It will be noted that the display of the sign does not mean that the Church Contacts are offering help. We have discovered that there is only one answer to be expected to the question "Do you need any help?" "No." It can be assumed that an enquirer who has a problem will find sympathetic assistance where the sign is shown, but the agreed policy is to refer spiritual problems to the Ministers, welfare problems to the appropriate social service. Church Contacts know that if there is any doubt I am available to advise what I feel is the appropriate course. The role of the "Contact", if need be, is to play the part of a friend.'

Miss Cornwall's account may be usefully concluded with the interpretation of the 'fish' sign which now appears on the inside of our visitors' introductory leaflet.

THE SIGN OF THE FISH

The information you need about the churches, Welfare Authorities and other facilities in the neighbourhood is available wherever you see the sign of the fish. This ancient sign symbolises:

CREED: The letters ICHTHUS (the Greek and New Testament word for 'fish') provide the initial letter of a simple Creed:
I Jesus, CH Christ, TH God's, U Son, S Saviour. The first three letters of the name CHRIST are also to be found in the X of the fish's tail (the Greek CH) and the 'crook' (the Greek R) which passes through it.

COMRADESHIP: The sign of the fish was sometimes used by the first Christians in time of persecution, to guide their friends to the pre-arranged house of meeting. Fish also appears in the depiction of early Christian communal meals. The sign is thus a reminder of the Presence of the Risen Christ, then and now, in quiet and in danger, and of the comradeship of all who meet at his table.

CARE: The practice of the early Church was to distribute to the sick and poor what was left over from the common meal. This spirit of sharing was enshrined in the story of the boy who entrusted his meal of bread and fish to Jesus. So this sign speaks of the desire of Christians of every age, not least our own, to share what they have with those in need. The Greek R may be seen as another symbol of caring for it looks rather like a shepherd's crook, reminder of One who said 'I am the Good Shepherd . . . and I lay down my life for the sheep. And other sheep I have . . . them also I must bring; and they shall hear my voice, and they shall become one flock, one shepherd.'

Look out for the sign of the fish. It is everywhere!

In April 1968, a new venture was made possible when three of the Addiscombe churches volunteered to meet the cost of displaying a poster in three bus shelters in our area. Bearing the now-familiar sign of the fish and the title 'The Addiscombe Group of Churches', the heading reads: 'This sign summarises the faith held by all Christian Churches'. At the foot of the poster it reads: 'For information about all local churches and other facilities available in this area ask at the sign of the fish or ring 654 2211.'

A lay leader of one of our churches once suggested that if he were to find time for the 'first-line' Home Mission he would have to be excused Sunday evening Worship. We have not, as yet, taken up his suggestion, but we note that it places the Church's witness in the street alongside the witness of the Church in corporate Worship . . . The question arises whether it would not give added significance to both Worship and Witness if, at the commencement of evening Worship several workers were to be sent out with the prayers of the whole congregation. We can no longer think of the Home Mission as an optional activity which may be withdrawn from the Church's programme when a few enthusiasts are no longer able to sustain it. We see it, rather, in the most intimate relationship with the Word faithfully preached and the Sacraments duly administered. We no longer see how the Church, in such urban areas as we have known, can produce a realistic translation of the Gospel into the terms of human need apart from the willingness of some to walk the streets, climb the stairs and knock on doors. The initiative of God does not seem to us to be faithfully communicated by a church which only waits for others outside to make the first move.

Some will remember the final lines of Studdert-Kennedy's poem entitled 'Indifference':

> The crowds went home and left the streets
> Without a soul to see,
> And Jesus crouched beneath a wall
> And cried for Calvary . . .

We see the Church under this condemnation, hurrying to its shelter and leaving the streets to the Master. We see the Church,

IN THE ROAD

along with the sects and the political parties, with no interest in the street beyond that of extracting men and women from it. We see the Church carrying a share of responsibility for the fragmentation of community. But we also have a vision of the Church repairing some of the damage, restoring threads of relationship, traversing the boundaries of sympathy, sharing the cost with its Master of walking the streets and bearing the message of reconciliation.

5. In the Church

THE Christian in the road needs to know that something is happening back inside his church. Without this assurance he may be attempting to represent to his neighbours a unity and a purpose untrue to the church as he knows it. But attitudes may be easier to change in relation to the church's role 'outside' than 'inside'. Alarm is not generally aroused until threat appears to the familiar pattern of one's own, denominational activities, based on one's own premises. In our experience the threat may be not as devastating as it sounds. The critics of established church activities do not satisfy us that they have much constructive to say in a given situation, or that, faced with a list of local church commitments (or committees) they would know where to start their knifing. Ironically the first requirement of re-appraisal may be recognition of what already exists—for instance, the ecumenical composition of a 'Methodist' Wives' Club. Primarily, we see the need for a new perspective: a seeing of the familiar within the life and witness of a whole Church (in practice, all the churches). Adminstratively, it may be necessary to form an exploratory group or an 'umbrella' committee; sometimes there will need to be a change of name; but such changes may be sufficient to arouse unease and hostility. In this chapter we describe some of the gestures which two churches have made towards the ideal of seeing the inside life of the Church as a whole. In terms of the Nottingham resolution[1] we describe ways in which we have tried to do things jointly or, if that has not been possible, to see that they are co-ordinated. In the nature

---

[1] See Chapter 2, page 19.

of things, such an experiment is largely confined to a partnership of two or three churches, in geographical proximity and within the working boundaries provided by—in our case—an Anglican Parish.

Following our 'Lund' covenant of September 1965, we found various practical ways of pledging our intention. Foremost among these was the exchange of observers at P.C.C. and L.M., but there were others. At the time the covenant was being considered, the Methodists were engaged in repainting their notice-boards. The titles approved by the trustees read: 'The Church in Addiscombe' with the denominational designation underneath, 'The Methodist Church'. The letterer managed to incorporate the *ichthus* and *chi-rho* device which was later adopted by the Addiscombe Group of Churches. In 1966 the Vicar and Minister were authorised to draft out and order our first joint headed correspondence paper. This we had printed in two forms, one for the use of adult organisations and one for the youth. The former reads

THE CHURCH IN ADDISCOMBE

The Parish Church of St. Mary Magdelene with Addiscombe Methodist Church

COMMUNITY SERVICE

Community Night	M.U. & Women's Social Hour
International Committee	Men's Forum
Sports and Badminton Clubs	Wives' Club (Afternoon)
Magdalene Players	Magdalene Women's Hour (Evening)

Appeals Committees   Teacher/Leader Training

Services for the Elderly   Confirmation/Membership
                                           Training

Car Service
                                 Marriage Preparation
Home Visiting   Groups

Nursery Play Group   Home Fellowships

                                 Service to Youth

Vicar: Minister:

(At the foot of the sheet it reads: Liaison with other Churches, Voluntary bodies and the Statutory Welfare Authorities.) The titles fall naturally into four short columns.

In accordance with the principle of 'seeing things whole', the Methodist Church Directory, produced in July 1966, bore the title 'The Church in Addiscombe—Methodist Sector'. At about the same time, the *Church of England Newspaper* began to appear beside the *Methodist Recorder* on the reading-desk in the Methodist Church foyer.

A feature of the life of the Addiscombe Methodist Church from 1958 to 1963 was the 'Wesley Guild'. This characteristic Methodist week-night meeting, dedicated to the fourfold objects of Consecration, Culture, Comradeship and Christian Service was a natural choice of activity for a church wishing to build up its own distinctive life after war and fire. The programme provided for Bible Study, Education in Christian mission and general cultural and recreational interests. It was supported by fifteen to thirty-five people, drawn, in the main, from the leadership of the Church. The Guild's usefulness was not unchallenged, and by 1964 several rival claims were apparent. Since it was understood that the Guild did not meet during the first seven days of each month, this being the Home Fellowship period, it could be claimed that the inter-church gatherings provided an adequate or preferable alternative to Guild devotional and study evenings. Similarly the House Visiting was making its claim upon available nights. The claim, deeply felt by some, of 'specialist' activities, such as the Intercessory Group and Teacher Training Classes, was equally pressing. Over and above these things was the generally acknowledged decline of the week-night meeting throughout suburbia. With considerations such as these in mind, the Methodists sought means of widening the scope and intention of the Guild and in May 1965, at a joint Leader's Meeting and Parochial Church Council, the Anglicans were formally invited to contribute members to a small working party to explore the possibility of an inter-church project. For the Anglicans the project represented a modest follow-up to some of the insights of the recent Parish study 'No Small Change'; for the Methodists a moment had come when it was no longer possible to give full content to their own declared 'Guild' objectives outside an ecumenical commitment.

The joint committee, consisting of three Anglicans and three Methodists, recommended that the Guild be developed as a 'Community Night', an open evening designed to meet ascertained wants and needs in the immediate neighbourhood. The June Leaders' Meeting gave authority to the Committee to proceed, subject only to the inclusion of the three 'statutory Methodist week-night meetings associated with Home and World Mission and Christian Citizenship.' This the Committee had no difficulty in accepting. A questionnaire was prepared and 3,200 copies distributed through the Parish Church Magazine net-work. Over the signature of Vicar and Minister, neighbours were invited to express their opinion about 'some form of Community Centre' and to indicate what facilities they would like to see made available. Facilities suggested included, Canteen, Lounge, Games Rooms, Reading Room, Music, Dancing, Drama; Discussion and Study Room, Quiet Room or Chapel. Forty replies were received, about half from people not personally known to us. A bewildering variety of interest was indicated; some seemed to contemplate half a dozen activities at the same time. Three-quarters of those replying desired the facilities of Canteen, Study and Chapel; about half were interested in the games and recreational opportunities. On the strength of this modest information we planned for an opening night at the end of September and despatched personal invitations to those who had taken the trouble to complete the questionnaire. About seventy people came.

The uncertainty which for some years had hung over the Methodist Guild did not disperse with the advent of the inter-church Community Night. From the small number of church people who gave thought to it—apart from agreeing that others might run it if they wanted to—we had several written contributions. A Methodist, whose letter ranged over numerous matters, was willing to agree that 'there is a need for a Church Community Centre'. 'In a limited sense each of our churches provide this. When we are united it will be possible to provide perhaps larger churches in each area with a fuller range of community activities . . . but our progress is limited by our progress towards unity.' With some justification he felt that at the present time we did not have the resources to do the thing well. A month after the opening, an Anglican contributor underlined the same point, pleading for more attractive premises. 'Walk round the premises very slowly looking with the eyes of strangers. Walk round them when no other human beings are about. Come in through the main gates. Observe the beauty of the new notice boards, the garden, the lively entrance-hall, all leading up to . . .

worship ... Feel afresh the impact of the cross ... This part of the building is shouting its hymn of praise. Now go and look at the rest of the building. God lives there too, and this is where we welcome newcomers. What is the rest of the building saying? Please could we have one piece of mouth-watering colour in every room, a picture, perhaps, or a gaily painted door? This is for the most part a prosperous neighbourhood and even old people are no longer inured to austerity in their homes. There must not be too sharp a contrast when they come to Community Centre, or they will not want to come at all, especially in the winter.' Contributions such as these were welcome, and we could have done with more. But at the beginning we could only say to our guests, 'These premises are not ideal, nor have we all the staff we need. But within reason, they are open for whatever you want to do; help us to make them a place of interest and friendship.'

The co-operation of two churches has not saved Community Night from staff shortage. But after two years it was firmly established and was meeting some of the needs envisaged. Some 'feature' or 'Lecture' evenings, such as those addressed by Dr. E. G. Parrinder of London University and Mr. Edwin Barker of the Church of England Board of Social Responsibility, were well attended and provided an audience double that which we might reasonably have expected within a denominational set-up. For adjacent churches to plan meetings of general Christian or public significance without reference to one another seems to us a wilful exploitation of human energy and good-will. A 'People Next Door' training group held from 9.0 to 9.45 p.m. was well attended, but strained our capacity for accurate time-keeping and over loaded the programme. A ten minute epilogue in church, conducted mainly by lay leaders, was a feature of the Night from its inception, and the continuation of other activities in other parts of the building at least gave us the satisfaction of knowing that the optional nature of all activities was known and accepted. The availability of a Minister has been one intention of the Night, and the Vicar, Minister or Church Army Captain have been on the premises as often as possible. At a period in the Spring of 1967, when it appeared that C.N. was becoming lopsided in favour of the lonely-elderly, a small teenage group, happier in the all-age organisation than the single-age Youth Club, began to grow in numbers and became a regular feature. The summer of 1967 saw an all-age attendance on nights offering no more than the 'basic' recreational facilities—something of a break-through in terms of our original objectives. Quality refreshments and improved premises and facilities, had their bearing on the establishment of Community Night, which has become basic to the Church's offer of friendship to its neighbours. In Chapter 6 we describe the part that C.N. has played in our cooperation with Welfare and Hospital authorities; its bearing on Methodist 'Departmentalism' is mentioned later in the chapter. One intention of the Night has been that a Minister should occasionally be available. It has been reported that the appearance of Vicar, Minister or Church Army Captain has provoked interest and enquiry from strangers.

Increasingly associated with Community Night was the work of the International Committee. Since the coming of the West Indian 'Church of God' to the Cherry Orchard Methodist premises, a group of Anglicans and Methodists (including three West Indians) has taken a particular interest in the well-being of our immigrant neighbours. Two of the English friends assisted for some time in the Pentecostal services of worship which would otherwise have had little contact with the established churches. The group has given generous help to individual families and formed close links of friendship. On the basis of Baptismal, Marriage and other records, and, not least, casual acquaintance, a card index of immigrant families was built up representing about one hundred family units. The Committee members accepted a pastoral role and have sought to keep in personal touch—not easy with a section of the population so often on the move. Immigrant families, of course, have in some cases come within the normal pastoral life of the Church, but without the help of a group of people willing to make the overseas new-comer their particular concern, personal contact would have been very limited indeed.

For two years the International Committee organised Saturday night 'International Evenings'. A beginning was made in May 1965 with the showing of a film about Jamaican Independence. Enthusiasm amply compensated for the loss of sound! Thereafter we held an evening at approximately three-monthly intervals, distributing 1,000 invitations on each occasion through channels available to us—immigrant homes, adult organisations, Youth Club, etc. The ingredients of each evening were simple: a musical 'group' or instrumentalist, a few items, sometimes impromptu, illustrating another culture, dancing, refreshments and brief family prayers. Evenings had a surprising way of gathering momentum and never failed to bring together people of different ages and races. At perhaps the most 'successful' evening about seventy-five were present, numbers being almost equally divided between Youth Club, Old Age Pensioners and West Indians. Anglo-Indians, Pakistanis, Ghanaians and Nigerians have also been present at the evenings. The 'Ceylonese' evening in February 1967 was a particularly successful merger of a Methodist 'Departmental' interest—in this case the Women's Work of the Missionary Society—with our local International concern. The most poignant memory was the evening when a close Nigerian friend, first encountered on a street corner, told us that two of his brothers had been massacred in the anti-Ibo uprisings in Northern Nigeria in July 1966. Our developing policy is to widen the personal-pastoral contact, to foster more inter-racial home fellowships, and to build up the international work as an integral part of Community Night. The occasional Saturday event serves to focus interest and to draw families out of a too-easy cultural confinement.

The organising Committee of Community Night was given the responsibility of co-ordinating all adult recreational activities, but so far has been pre-occupied with its own organisation. However, the C.N. Notice Board offers Badminton, Drama and the rest as 'associated Activities' and we see a slow breakdown of isolationist habits of thought. The Magdalene Badminton Club has been able to make emergency use of the Methodist court and the Magdalene Players have had the freedom of Community night to seek out fresh interest and talent. 'Appeals' committees continue to operate as independent bodies each with their own structure of efforts and their own net-work of collectors: but the general secretary of C.N. is now applying his professional experience to possible rationalisation. Three or four organisations depending largely upon 'church' personnel are able to make more efficient and less-demanding use of their man-power by this kind of co-operation.

The Services for the Elderly and Handicapped, begun during the ministry of Ernest's predecessor, Fred Hollinghurst, have gradually found their place within the inter-church Community Service. Over a period of three years, a link was established with around a hundred elderly and handicapped persons. These desired to share in the corporate worship of the church but for various reasons were unable. In most cases transport for them was essential; in many the persons concerned were unable to sit through a full-length service in any comfort. About twenty car drivers, who now include Anglicans and Congregationalists, made themselves available to the organisers, and each month about sixty elderly or invalid people are conveyed from an area several miles around to 'Saturday Service'. Experiment has shown which cars are most suitable for particular people and mutual confidence has grown up between drivers and passengers. Nearly all the ministers in the area have consented to conduct the service which normally consists of three hymns, Bible Reading, Prayer and an Address, lasting in all about thirty-five minutes. Coffee and biscuits then follow before transport home at 12 noon. Organisation is divided between the Invitations Secretary and the Transport Organiser. Invitations are posted each month, a return slip being provided to indicate whether transport is required. Secretaries go to the extra trouble of completing and dispatching 'Fellowship of Worship' cards[2] giving persons unable to attend the opportunity of pondering the hymns sung and the Scripture read. Transport runs to an established pattern, but has to be flexible enough to incorporate the steady changeover of personnel, as those no longer able to attend are replaced by new-comers—often commended to us by the House Visitors. When our one (Methodist) mini-bus has not been available, our Roman Catholic colleague has readily offered us his own. On the first occasion that Father McKenna, of Addiscombe Roman Catholic Church, conducted the service, Ernest received a letter of protest from Belfast; but the members of the congregation, some of whom have enjoyed no regular Christian Worship for years, take a delight in the ecumenical ministry. The hard-pressed car service has taken other responsibilities, including a summer (Community Night) car drive and the collection and return of a pupil at the Royal School for the Blind twenty-five miles away.

Women's organisations, beyond sharing the same headed correspondence paper, have not established formal links and we see their work as complementary. The Mothers' Union

[2] Available from the Epworth Press.

basis of membership would exclude some of those incorporated into the Methodist organisations and times of meeting relate to differing circumstances. Groups differ in the degree of their church commitment—say from M.U. to Wives' Club—but we see each within the same context of Christian fellowship. Mother's Union, Social Hour, Wives' Club and Women's Own (Cherry Orchard) each have between forty and seventy on their books with attendances around forty. Joint gatherings have become a feature of the programmes and consultation between the Leaders is normal, but we have valued the distinct life and spirit of each group and have not envisaged permanently larger entities. The remarkable 'Unity Club', meeting in the Roman Catholic Hall, is an interesting exception in terms of size and leadership. Catering for men as well as for women (although the former are much in the minority) it places a ceiling of 220 on membership and is compelled to have a waiting list. The free and recreational nature of the activities and a system of sub-dividing into 'tables' each with its own 'hostess', encourages close friendship and deep mutual interest; we are not, therefore, able to claim that the smaller, traditional women's meetings necessarily promote a closer sense of community. Leadership and organisation in the Unity Club is fully inter-denominational.[3] We observe, then, that thanks to churches and other voluntary organisations, the women of our area have a choice of meeting-place on any day, Monday to Thursday inclusive, with Unity Club each Friday. A few share the distinction of three or four allegiances.

The much more limited Men's organisation was from its inception an ecumenical venture and did much to create the understanding which led to other things becoming possible.

[3] See also Chapter 1, page 12.

IN THE CHURCH

The Anglican and Methodist men were first called together in the autumn of 1954 as part of the 'follow-up' of the Evanston Assembly.[4] At the first meeting the Rev. Gordon Strutt spoke on 'Faith and Order', and in succeeding months the men engaged in other studies arising from the Assembly Report. In October 1956, the Addiscombe 'United Men's Forum' was constituted as the united men's meeting of the Parish Church of St. Mary Magdalene and the two Methodist churches of Addiscombe and Cherry Orchard. Men's Forum met six times a year, from October to April, moving in rotation around the three churches and was responsible for the arrangement of the United Parish Holy Week Service.[5] For ten years the programme of the Forum was related to the Church and its faith in the ecumenical era. This 'learning together' in growing friendship and the close association of laymen and ministers laid a foundation upon which later work could be built—the Home Fellowships, the House Visiting and the other jointly-administered projects. In 1967 it was agreed that the Forum had achieved the purpose for which it had come into being and that it should cease to operate as a separate unit. It was felt that recreational objects would be better served by Community Night and the educational by forming a link with the St. Mildred's Church of England Men's Society. Seeing the life of the Church as a whole saved us from the perpetuation of an activity 'for old times' sake' whilst preserving a facility for those seeking it.

The headed correspondence paper prepared for the use of the Youth organisations was similar to that for the 'Community Service' and read as follows:

---

[4] The Second Assembly of the World Council of Churches, Evanston, Illinois, U.S. 1954 *To stay together is not enough, we must go forward.*
[5] See Chapter 9, page 144.

The Church in Addiscombe

The Parish Church of St. Mary Magdalene with Addiscombe Methodist Church

Service to Youth

Baby and Toddlers Creches	Youth Sports and Badminton Clubs
Sunday Schools and Junior Church	
	Magdalene Players
Young People's Groups	Magdalene Singers
Scouts, Guides, Cubs, Brownies	Teacher/Leader Training
Juniors & Inters Clubs	Confirmation/Membership Training
Magnets and Nomads Youth Clubs	Community Service

Vicar: Minister:

(At the foot of the sheet it reads: Liaison with Church Youth Departments and the London Borough of Croydon Youth Authority.) The titles are also in four parallel columns.

The joint Youth Service was anticipated under the pressure of war by the '14—20 Club', so named after the requirements of the then Board of Education respecting the social and physical development of boys and girls between the ages of fourteen and twenty who had ceased full time education.[6]

[6] Board of Education Circular No. 1486, 27 November 1939.

Meeting on the Methodist premises—which at that time included a gymnasium—the Club was run by lay men and women of the two churches. It continued until the fire of 1948 and thereafter, until 1953, in a local school and other premises. But the mood was now for the creation of denomination-orientated youth work, and Addiscombe, like many hundreds of Methodist churches throughout the country, built it up afresh under the auspices of the Methodist Association of Youth Clubs. From 1956 to 1966 the Methodist work, on the Cherry Orchard premises, became a joint activity of the two local Methodist Societies. It was during the latter part of this decade that, with the encouragement of the local Youth Department, the work became largely open, with as many as 150 teenagers on the books and attendances twice a week of around eighty. This development led to a reconsideration of the Church's youth policy and the decision of the Cherry Orchard Church to establish its own, church-orientated, youth activity. Those convinced of the Church's responsibility in the field of open youth work were left looking for new premises, and with the knowledge of the joint P.C.C. and L.M., in May 1965, three sets of church premises, Anglican and Methodist, were surveyed in the company of the Croydon Youth Officer. Slowly our minds turned to the dilapidated Oval Church Hall, for long an uncertain factor in the Parish Church situation, but still in use for Sunday School, Badminton and the Anglican 'Magnets' Youth Club. An exploratory Committee representing Anglican and Methodist youth clubs examined the possibilities in the light of statutory grant-aid and came up with a recommendation which in outline was approved by the Methodist Leaders' Meeting in June 1966 and two days later by the Parochial Church Council. While the immediate concern was for the establishment of the Youth Club work, the recommendations envisaged the co-ordination of all the youth work of the two churches. The resolutions were as follows:

THE CHURCH IN ADDISCOMBE SERVICE TO YOUTH

1. That the youth work of St. Mary Magdalene Parish Church and the Addiscombe Methodist Church be integrated under the name of the 'Church in Addiscombe—Service to Youth'.

2. That the said Service to Youth shall combine the open facilities at present offered by the Magnets and Nomads Youth Clubs, together with the specialised activities for, or including, the fourteen–twenty-one age group: e.g. Youth Badminton, Youth Drama, Cricket, and Football Clubs.

3. That the said Service to Youth at present cater for the fourteen–twenty-one age group, but be ready to incorporate the eleven–fourteen group as and when this becomes desirable and possible.

4. That the said Service to Youth aim to provide a seven-day-a-week programme for youth, with a minimum of four evenings weekly at two and a half hours per evening for not less than forty-two weeks in the year.

5. That the combining organisations continue to operate as sectional activities with their own sub-committees responsible to the Management Committee.

6. That the Management Committee of the said Service to Youth consists of:

a. The Ministers and Clergy of the participating churches one of whom shall be *ex officio* chairman of the Committee as arranged between them.

b. Four adult representatives from each of the two churches concerned. Appointment to be by Annual vote of the respective church councils each June.

c. Co-opted persons with special qualifications, as decided by the Committee.

IN THE CHURCH

7. That the Management Committee be responsible for advising the two churches on the most advantageous use of the premises available, with particular reference to the youth work.

8. That the Management Committee be responsible for the appointment of:

Club Leaders on the nomination of the representative church council.

Sectional Leaders on the nomination of the sections.

General Secretary of the Service to Youth.

Treasurer of the Service to Youth.

9. That the Management Committee be responsible for the general policy of the Service to Youth, in accordance with its agreed standards and aims, and for the proper allocation of monies received from the Education Committee and such other funds as may be received from the respective sections and other sources.

10. That the Management Committee meet at least twice each year, and be responsible for the calling of an Annual General Meeting uniting all sections.

11. That the Management Committee be responsible for making application to the Croydon Education Committee (Youth Sub-Committee) for Grant-aid and for full liaison with the Local Authority and the respective churches.

12. SCOPE AND INTENTION

That the said Service to Youth seek to provide for social, recreational, educational and spiritual needs of all young people in the area served; to encourage its members to play a full part in the life of Club and community and to engage in at least one purpose-orientated activity (either within or outside the Service to Youth) each week; to set explicit Christian standards of respect for property, people and God, and to commend them, as far as possible, by example rather than precept;

to make devotional activities, as agreed by the Club or sectional Committees, a matter of choice rather than compulsion, and church attendance a matter of personal invitation rather than a condition of membership.

The creation of the Service to Youth in 1966—a natural concomitant of the Community Service—illustrated the way in which the development of the 'Lund' principle may be encouraged by practical necessity. The Methodists were without a home for a two-night open Youth Club and Ernest shared the view of those who saw this as an essential piece of Christian neighbourhood service. The Anglicans, on the other hand, were facing a long-delayed decision respecting the Oval Parish Hall. Sale would realise a small amount of much-needed capital and save the P.C.C. the embarrassment of costly repairs. At the same time Neville and others were aware of strong feeling that the Parish Church should not pull out from a strategic position at the west end of the Parish. The two problems found a common solution in the uniting of our work. Which of the two churches 'gained' the more by the agreement is entirely speculative: the satisfactory thing is that two problems found an immediate solution within an imaginative and promising enterprise. The Methodist Youth work not merely found a home but a place within a more diverse pattern of youth activity; the Anglican Church Hall not merely became economically self-supporting, but a greatly enlivened centre of Christian service. In 1961 there had been correspondence between the Parish Church and the Youth Authority which had come to nothing.

In its first year of working, the Service to Youth Management Committee was pre-occupied with the task of establishing the Oval premises on an economic footing. The Methodist 'Nomads' Youth Club had moved in during September, but financial arrangements had not been worked out and were dependent on full-scale grant-aid being available from the London Borough of Croydon through its Education Youth Sub-Committee. The Anglican 'Magnets' joined forces with the Methodist 'Nomads' and activities eligible for aid resolved themselves into two 'affect-orientated' nights (the Open Youth Club) and two 'purpose-orientated' nights (the Youth Badminton and the Table Tennis Section). On this basis grants were eventually agreed with the Authority, respecting the financial year 1 April 1967 to 31 March 1968. Severe limitation of capital for repair work demanded the maximum use of voluntary labour and during 1967 Club members dismantled and re-built forty feet of dangerous boundary wall, repaired the kitchen floor, decorated the toilets, installed electric radiant heaters and began work on creating a lounge and leader's office in the south 'transept'. Meanwhile, urgent roof repairs were effected and plans were laid for bringing the premises up to a sound condition within another financial year. In early 1968 an invitation was delivered to homes in the immediate neighbourhood inviting our neighbours to open evenings at the church Youth Centre. By this time it had become desirable for the joint Management Committee to take full responsibility for the hall, and, at the suggestion of the P.C.C. the existing Hall Management Committee handed over its responsibilities to the joint body. Under five heads of agreement the joint committee was given full and exclusive use of the premises for a period of five years and made responsible for day to day repairs and all out-goings. The premises were to be used for such purposes as were mutually agreed by the two churches. It was envisaged that the premises should be self-supporting, but in the event of a deficit the two churches were to take an equal share of responsibility. Our joint project was an exercise in working together with the Local Authority as well as with one another.

Long before the formation of the 'Service to Youth' our Sunday School staffs had become accustomed to meet with one another and in 1964, on Anglican initiative, they had before them a proposal for the unification of the work among senior children, as from the first Sunday in 1965. This proposal proved premature. Anglican Sunday School and Methodist Junior Church were meeting at different times, the Methodists being in process of changing to a morning period coinciding with adult worship. The age range of the Anglican 'Pathfinders' (twelve to eighteen) involved two Methodist departments, Senior (eleven to fourteen) and Young People's Fellowship (fifteen to eighteen). A problem of greater concern to the Methodists was raised by different teaching-methods, and they were unwilling to contemplate a departure from the principle of the small teaching unit. Consultation with the national Methodist Youth Department confirmed their reluctance to make any hasty change. On the Anglican side it was felt by some that the Methodists did not 'mean business'. For three years, therefore, the matter was deferred. However, the Anglicans had made clear their willingness to consider the use of the British Lessons Council syllabus (the basis of the Methodist and Free Church graded teaching material) and the announcement of the new Council syllabus commencing October 1968 suggested that the time had come for renewed exploration together. The new B.L.C. syllabus, the work of a research group set up in 1963, incorporates the results of much current thinking on Religious Education and contributes to the possibility envisaged in one of the resolutions of 'Nottingham':

'We request the British Council of Churches to re-examine in consultation with the National Sunday School Union, the Scottish Sunday School Union, and similar bodies, the possibility of extending the work of the existing Education and Youth Departments of the Council so as to cover the

IN THE CHURCH

member churches' education of children up to the age of fifteen.'[7] Our Sunday School staffs have kept the objective in mind that we should find our way to a common teaching syllabus.

Our first joint Sunday School staff meetings were not without results. An open invitation remained to the Methodist Junior Church to participate in the long-established youth Summer Camps run by St. Mary Magdalene's. The Methodist Junior Club filled a gap in our leisure-time provision for the eight to eleven age group and it was agreed that Church of England children should be free to attend. It was acknowledged that, if possible, we should help each other in staffing problems and the Methodists recognised their debt to Anglican helpers in the leadership of their uniformed organisations. Our teachers have shared in training conferences and anticipate more joint training in connection with the B.L.C. syllabus. Recently we have arranged for mutual representation on our respective Youth Councils, whilst the six-monthly Parish Family services at St. Mary Magdalene's are regarded as part of the Christian education of the children in our care. Significant in the development of our thinking was the President's 'At Home' held in connection with the Croydon and District Sunday School Union in November 1964. On this occasion Neville was able to speak to one hundred representatives of Free Church Schools in the Borough on the subject: 'The End of the Denominational Sunday School'. He put the work of the Sunday School into the context of a Church entrusted with the Gospel of reconciliation. He envisaged the uniting of the work of contiguous churches in three stages: 1. the free and frank exchange of information; 2. the consideration of the task in relation to the area served and the best use of staff and

[7] The National Sunday School Union is now the National Christian Education Council and a sponsor of the work of the British Lessons Council.

premises; 3. the organisation of the work so that the churches will be seen as the Church in the given area. We were surprised at the measure of agreement evoked. General approval was voiced concerning united staff meetings, departmental consultation, a common syllabus, the pastoral care of children slipping between one denomination and another and the desirability of visits to Sunday Schools by Ministers of different denominations. Within our own churches we felt that these points were largely taken and that they were becoming part of our understanding of colleagueship.

At the Sunday School gathering Neville astonished some of his hearers by saying that the St. Mary Magdalene confirmation candidates and teachers accompanied him to the Jewish Synagogue, the Roman Mass, the Friends Meeting House and the Methodist Preaching Service. While Neville has explored these avenues of ecumenical training more consistently than Ernest, we have both accepted that membership training is something that we do ecumenically and in part together. We have usually arranged for the other to take sessions of our membership training course and we have tried to see that the 'other' church is represented at Confirmation or Reception Services.[8] Another field of cooperation in training has been courses for engaged couples. With the ready co-operation of the Croydon and District Marriage Guidance Council we have been able to offer two short discussion-courses each year to all couples engaged to be married in one of our churches. The majority have accepted the invitation and been deeply grateful for the experience. The members of one of the more recent courses decided that they must meet together again—six months after their marriages.

The consideration of 'in-church' activities should properly include Worship, Ministerial and Lay Colleagueship and Lay Conferences. These we have left to three separate chapters.

[8] See Chapter 9, p. 149.

Meanwhile we would observe that the re-thinking of the internal life of the church is a major pre-requisite of the Church's cooperation with and service to others. We see the possibilities of the Church's participation in the society around it as almost unlimited, but only as it is willing to see itself as a whole and to bear the scrutiny of people who are uninterested by claims which bear no relation to performance.

6. In with Others

OBEDIENCE in Christian service has brought us together with others as inevitably as it brought us together as churches. By 'others' we mean, principally, the statutory and voluntary welfare services. As in our relationship with our neighbour churches, so in our relationship with these agencies, the principle of 'recognition' has been fundamental.[1] Even a cursory knowledge of their work has made intolerable that popular Christian conceit that only 'Christians' can offer service of a Christian quality. We have had to abandon an unwarranted pride for the humble recognition that much 'secular' service is more dedicated than our own. This we have been compelled to recognise, not least, in the enormous field of central and local Government enterprise. We reflect upon the extraordinary provision made by our own London Borough for the mentally and physically handicapped, or the time which a Schools sub-Committee may spend on the interests of a single child, and ask, where is the Presence of Christ in this situation if not here? We cannot reconcile an attitude of 'non-recognition' with the biblical view of God and his world.[2] We observe how the apostles could commend secular authority as deriving from God[3]; it is strange that Christians should withold a similar recognition from government which is often as remarkable for its compassion as for its authority. We therefore see the Church in each place morally bound to keep its life open to the affairs of the community in which it lives and to the concerns of those who are its appointed servants.

[1] See Chapter 2, p. 18.
[2] See Bibliography.
[3] 1 Peter 2:13–17, etc.

IN WITH OTHERS

An exercise suggested for Home Fellowships during the winter 1967-8 was the study of several Borough Council agendas in the light of the Bible. Except through the interest or the daily vocation of individuals, our churches have no obvious association with the work of the Finance Committee (unless they happen to be waiting for a grant), nor with the formidable alphabetical list which includes: Civil Defence and Public Services, Establishment, Halls, Highways and Works, Libraries, Parks, Cemeteries and Allotments, Planning and Water. In the public mind we would certainly be associated with the cemeteries; but why not with parks and allotments as well? *Il me fait reposer dans des parcs herbeux.*[4] *La Sainte Bible* suggests a beginning for a biblical appraisal! The solemn theme of disaster-survival, the every-day one of weights and measures, the appointment and work of the municipal officers, the use of the Public Halls (would the hanging of anti-Vietnam War paintings be detrimental to relations with our American visitors?), the routing of the new roads and the disposal of the sewerage, the purchase of books and trees and bulbs, the architecture of a twentieth century town centre and the age-long urgency of water supplies: each theme demands its own biblical study within the context of God's will for the community which the local Church is there to serve. On Christian conscience and Public Finance (which heads every Council agenda) we have not read a more searing comment than that of the *New Christian*[5] on the publication of the findings of the Aberfan tribunal: 'The officials of the National Coal Board mentioned in the report . . . are not wicked men who deliberately set out to destroy a school full of children . . . The ugly colliery tips throughout the country are a symbol of an industry which has been required by society to extract the maximum coal at the minimum cost and care little for the consequences. Those who have never complained about the

[4] Psalm 23:2.   [5] *New Christian*, No. 49, 10 August 1967.

size of their fuel bills will be in the best position to judge those who are now carrying the blame at Aberfan.'

Our belated attempts to recognise the Christian significance of the work of 'others' was prompted, in part, by their recognition of us. Strangely, this came without any approaches on our part such as those undertaken so thoroughly by the Birmingham Council of Churches in their 'Social Responsibility Project'.[6] Soon after Dorothy Cornwall became our Group Organiser in 1966, social workers discovered us as a working proposition and the telephone began to ring. It was our worry, not that of the professional welfare workers, that our operational efficiency was dependent, almost entirely, upon our unpaid Group Organiser and that our Road Warden net-work, in much of the area, was in tatters. That our services were discovered and used we attribute to 1. the efficiency and tact of our organiser, 2. the willingness of church members 'on the spot' (whatever their denomination) to respond to the special call upon their time and sympathy, and 3. the non-denominational nature of our undertaking. The breakdown of one Church 'Good Neighbour' scheme was attributed by a correspondent to 'an absurd denominational pre-occupation'.

A weakness in our present situation is that links with statutory bodies are still largely dependent upon the personal and unofficial approach of individual welfare workers. The departure of one officer from one department might leave us without informed or sympathetic contact. On the other hand, we have not been anxious to become too closely involved in local government departments wrestling with their own internal problems of coordination in the Welfare field. Our limited experience of partnership has already underlined for us the need anticipated in the 1968 Social Work (Scotland) bill for many different welfare functions to be combined 'under one roof'. At the moment of writing, the Seebohm

[6] See Bibliography.

Committee,[7] which may recommend a similar structure for England, is still awaited. In the absence of formal ties with statutory Welfare, we have found it essential to be formally associated, as a Group of Churches, with liaison bodies such as the Guild of Social Service and the Croydon Association for Mental Health.

The level at which the Church has usually been brought in alongside 'others' is at 'grass-roots'—where every human 'problem' comes to earth in a particular person living at a particular address in a particular neighbourhood. At this level, departmental distinctions may be confusing and inapplicable, but, for convenience, we attempt to illustrate the work in which we have been involved from five general fields of statutory service: Children, Education, Health, Housing and Welfare. We have associated voluntary agencies with the statutory as it seemed appropriate.

In general, our association with the Children's Department has been limited to a few consultations each year, perhaps regarding a child or an unmarried mother; links with the Croydon Association for Moral Welfare have been of a similar nature. But the Children's Department raises several issues for the Christian conscience, for instance, in the claims of fostering or adoption: here we find that, particularly through the Wives' Clubs, the Church offers an 'open ear' to the concerns of the Children's officers. It was from the Children's Department that we received an enquiry whether the churches had considered organising a good used-clothing store with the special object of helping young mothers. All enquiries have not been so easy to answer: the excellently-run Y.W.C.A. Nearly-New shop was open twice a week at St. Mary Magdalene, the Friday opening-time coinciding with the Infant Welfare clinic at the Methodist premises one hundred and fifty yards away.

[7] Published 23 July 1965.

The complexity of our channels of information and 'referral' is illustrated by the case of an unsupported mother for whom our help was sought, in the first place, by the Children's Department. Unofficially it had been discovered that unless private transport could be found, one of the two children would be unable to benefit from treatment at a Children's Hospital in a neighbouring Borough. A few weeks later, a third child was born, and this time it was the Medical Social Worker of the Maternity Hospital asking if we could provide transport home for mother and baby. The Health Visitor at our local Clinic next came into the picture: 'Did we know about so-and-so?' At the same time a commendation arrived from a Curate a few miles away. These were the beginnings of a permanent pastoral relationship.

Traditionally, most churches in the Group take an interest in nearby homes for unmarried mothers, the Anglicans, more especially, in Glazier House, run by the Croydon Association for Moral Welfare, the Methodists in their mother and baby home at Streatham. Church support for these voluntary agencies is invariably inter-denominational, and churches of all denominations seem to play some part in the life of the independent 'Mission of Hope' in South Croydon, which maintains a complex of Babies' Nurseries, Children's Homes and a Maternity Home. The Methodists still take the chief responsibility for local collections on behalf of the National Childrens' Home, but support both for collections and annual Fête is given without regard to denominational loyalties.

Under the constitution of the new London Boroughs, which came into operation on the first of April, 1965, three church traditions were given the opportunity of nominating representatives to the Schools Sub-committee of the Education Committee. A ministerial trio, Anglican, Free Church and Roman Catholic, were appointed and the Council of Churches, having *per se* no right of nomination, has recognised these three as representing the interests of the churches in the Borough. Work preparatory to the adoption of a new 'agreed syllabus' of religious education has brought together a great number of interested people from both schools and churches, while persons with special qualifications have had the opportunity of serving on working parties or acting in an advisory capacity. The colleagueship of ministers of almost all denominations in all areas of the Borough, and not least in Addiscombe, has greatly facilitated cooperation of this nature between the churches and the Education Authority. Equally significant is the exploration of local School-Church relationships and the question of the possible deployment of suitably qualified ministers in the schools. Reports, available only to members of the Education committees, concerning the numbers and disposition of 'immigrant' children[8] in the Croydon Schools, alerted us to the approximate numbers of coloured teenagers whom we may shortly expect in one of our nearby 'catchment' areas and made it possible for our International and Service to Youth committees to begin advance study and planning. In Addiscombe, as in other parts of the Borough, we have been glad to welcome class 'projects' involving visits to local churches; we hope that, in some measure, we have been able to present a picture of churches involved in a single task.

Though the churches, as such, are not formally represented on the Youth Sub-committee, our interests are cared for by the representatives of Church-sponsored youth organisations and by general knowledge of the Church's interest in this field. Cooperation with the local Youth Department has become almost indispensable for churches seriously concerned to serve the needs of youth outside church conformity. The (then) Board of Education Circular to local authorities, written under the pressures of war, is still of primary significance to the relationship of Church and State in the field of the

[8] A loose term for the children of immigrant parents.

Youth Service. 'Now, as never before, there is a call for the close association of local education authorities and voluntary bodies in full partnership in a common enterprise; nor need this entail any loss of prestige or individuality on either side.[9] The 1945 Ministry of Education Report of the Youth Advisory Council justly refers to the impetus given to church and voluntary work in the field by 'the greater interest shown by statutory authority'.[10] The acceptance of voluntary organisations as 'equal partners' with statutory bodies[11] and the continuing acceptance—as by our own local authority—of the voluntary principle, challenges the sincerity of the churches in their professed desire to serve the community and represents a confidence in us which we are not sure has been fully deserved. We cannot escape the conclusion that Christian understanding of the objectives and methods of youth work have been informed, in part, by the insights of the State service.

The churches in Addiscombe, and especially the 'twosome' of St. Mary Magdalene and Addiscombe Methodist, have valued the opportunity of planning their youth work in consultation with the youth officers and are engaged in the cooperative venture of the Oval Youth Centre described in the preceding chapter. Not the least valuable feature has been the ability to plan within a total picture of need and provision. (The population of Croydon under the age of eighteen is expected to be about 100,000 in 1971.[12]) A much larger venture in Church–State cooperation has been undertaken at the Parchmore Road Methodist Church, Thornton Heath, where existing church premises have been re-modelled to serve youth within the context of a Church, Youth and Community

---

[9] Board of Education Circular No. 1486, 27 November 1939.
[10] Report of the Youth Advisory Council, 1945, p. 5.
[11] The Charities Act, 1960.
[12] Report of Children's Committee, 22 May 1967.

Centre. Already we are finding exchange of experience between ourselves and Thornton Heath of mutual benefit.

Facilities for Further Education (or Adult Education) have had a significant bearing on our work. The annual brochure of leisure-time courses, issued by the Borough Education Committee, is offered on our book-stalls and is particularly linked with Community Night. As with 'open' Youth Club, so with 'open' Community Night, we have tried to see the church-provided meeting points as a potential watershed contributing to numerous streams of more specialised activity. (We would like to see the 'neighbourhood' grouping and the 'common interest' grouping—where people may be drawn from widely scattered neighbourhoods—as complementary rather than conflicting.) Both our Group Organiser and the colleague who volunteered in 1968 to work with her, attended the London University Extra-mural four-year course in Sociology at Croydon Technical College. Another of our workers benefited from the twelve-week course, 'Play with a Purpose' designed for workers in the field of pre-school nursery play groups. We found that neither the Youth nor the Further Education Sub-committees made direct provision for pre-marriage training and we have informed them of courses arranged by the local churches in association with the Croydon and District Marriage Guidance Council.

In the field of Health[13] the churches have many historic and traditional associations and Croydon is no exception. For several years we have had a small link with the Public Health Department through the pre-school Nursery Play Group run by voluntary helpers on several mornings each week at the Cherry Orchard Methodist premises. Another group is centred on the premises at St. Mildred's. We are under increasing pressure to provide more comprehensive facilities, particularly from 'immigrant' mothers, but are only

[13] See also Chapter 9 on services of Healing.

at the point of exploratory consultation. The emerging interest of the Education authority in this work may prove a significant factor in future development.

Familiar to mothers throughout the country is the use of Church premises as Infant and Child Welfare clinics. Short of purpose-built premises, our Addiscombe Methodist Church offers pleasant accommodation, and the provision of attractive literature in waiting room or foyer, including information about all local churches, has provided a natural link between a Welfare service and the local Church. As and when staff time-tables permit, we hope to relate the Health Department's Toddlers' Club (for all mothers of small children) more closely to the Church in Addiscombe's Wives' Club—this is likely to be of mutual benefit. A friendly relationship between local ministers and the staff of the clinic has been helpful in cases where commendation to minister or church worker is indicated; confidence is created by the knowledge that commendation is, in effect, to an inter-church Ministerial Staff rather than simply to the minister of the church on whose premises the clinic happens to be held. The same premises also provide the head-quarters of the St. John Ambulance Brigade (Addiscombe) Division and the East Croydon and Addiscombe Nursing Division. Thus with voluntary as well as with statutory organisations, relationships are being built up which, we believe, enrich understanding of the Christian service in which we are respectively engaged.

In July 1966, Neville was approached by the organiser-manager of Croydon Industries for the Disabled regarding the Crosfield Industrial Unit in Cherry Orchard Road. The unit has for some years provided work for mentally and physically handicapped persons, some of whom are later able to undertake normal industrial work. Faced with inadequate premises and the need to expand workshop facilities into a hall hitherto used for club and recreational purposes, the organiser enquired whether the Parish Church could help *a.* with the provision of temporary, alternative premises for the one-night-a-week club and *b.* with a small number of reliable club helpers. Help might include taking a retarded person through a simple child-reader, playing a game of dominoes or teaching the guitar; but the essential requirement would be interest and absolute reliability. Neville replied that he was unable to act without consultation with his Methodist and Roman Catholic colleagues. We conferred and felt confident that our churches could rise to the occasion. The confidence, however, was not altogether justified. Two groups of our people visited the Crosfield club, several making firm offers of help. But the church premises which we hoped might be available did not materialise and the club and recreational activities were moved to a new centre on Purley Way, far removed from our area of the Borough and not practically accessible to our own helpers. Crosfield has remained within the interest of the local churches and at one of them was made the subject of a Sunday evening Concern service, the deputy organiser describing the Unit's work to the congregation.

In *Parishes with a Purpose*[14] Neville has already described something of the Croydon Branch of the Samaritans—for the help of those tempted to suicide or despair. Upwards of twenty members of our own congregations have been accepted into this service since its inception in Croydon about five years ago. Though not generally known in our congregations as Samaritan workers, their experience has had an undoubted influence on the Church's understanding of its own pastoral care. The capacity to be a good listener, the ability to keep counsel, the preparedness to offer friendship without overemotional involvement and without strings—these qualities have contributed to the pastoral motive and method of the whole Church. Needless to say, Samaritan helpers and others

[14] Page 24.

with experience gained with the Association for Moral Welfare, Marriage Guidance, the Women's Royal Voluntary Service, etc., have been of invaluable help when people with particular needs have been commended to the friendship of Community Night or some other church-sponsored organisation.

The formation of the Croydon Association for Mental Health in 1967, the appointment of Mr. H. P. Muller as Coordinator of the Croydon Voluntary Aid project, and, finally, the opening of Rees House in 1968, brought us in a much more immediate way into the field of mental health. Mr. Muller came as one of the 'observers' to our Addiscombe/Shirley study conference in March 1968 and was able to outline to one hundred and twenty workers from twelve churches his plans for the participation of 'ordinary' people in helping those who suffer from mental stress and handicap. Persons reluctant to become involved in a field understandably left to the professional were reassured by the practical nature of the work requested and, not least, by Mr. Muller's confidence in 'common-sense' attitudes. Rees House, providing a day clinic for patients returning from hospital to their homes, reinforced our conviction that the Church had to be fully involved. The clinic was on our door-step and was asking for help which it was within the capacity of many of our members to give: helping patients to get back to their domestic routine by cooking a dinner, dress-making, gardening, caring for children while parents receive treatment . . . We felt we should be formally associated with the Croydon Association of Mental Health and with the Voluntary Aid project and we were sure that the realistic thing was to affiliate, not as individual churches, but as a working Group. In February 1968 the ministerial staff authorised the Group Organisers (now two in number) to recruit a Mental Health 'Special Aid' group and the first volunteers were quickly forthcoming. Instilling confidence in volunteers was the knowledge that at

IN WITH OTHERS

all times a social worker is on duty at Rees House and is available to the untrained worker for consultation. Training sessions, organised by the Association for Mental Health, had already been attended by some of our workers.

In the field of mental health, two of our 'door-to-door' visitors one evening stumbled across a need of which they (and most of us) had previously been unaware. They found themselves talking to a lady in early middle life who had scarcely been outside her own door for seventeen years. The visitors felt that their 'contact' could not await the Report-back meeting in ten days time and immediately shared their concern with the Group Organiser. Since that evening in early 1968 'Agoraphobia' has become part of our awareness of need among the people around us. Ernest has been welcomed at a house-gathering of the 'Open Door'—an informal organisation providing self-help through group therapy—and we have been able to make church premises (Roman Catholic and Methodist) available to the association for larger social functions. Visiting has revealed other cases of similar need and there has been mutual referral between Church and 'Open Door'. Our first contact-person, the discovery of our first-line visitors, wrote: 'it's a great help to us all to know someone has at last noticed us "Aggies" . . . our members are on your door-step.' Another sufferer wrote: 'If there is anyone living nearby who doesn't seem to go out, it would help if people offered, now and again, to do a bit of shopping for her. That is enough.'

The contribution of the Church to the Housing situation seems almost infinitesimal in comparison with the need and with the statistics of the Housing Department; but we believe that its importance lies in more than statistics. A 'This is Your Life' programme on T.V. led to a meeting between the Rev. E. Nevill Phair, Vicar of St. Mildred's and Major Richard Carr-Gomm, founder of the Abbeyfield Society.[15] Looking

[15] See Addresses, p. 164.

over the first Abbeyfield house in Bermondsey, Nevill saw how the same principle of combating human loneliness could be applied to the Parish he knew in Addiscombe. The result was that exploratory talks were held with interested people and Abbeyfield Addiscombe Society Limited was incorporated in July 1963. Six churches were involved in the venture, two Anglican (St. Mildred's and St. Mary Magdalene), three Methodist (Ernest's two, plus Shirley) and the Addiscombe Roman Catholic Church. The cost of purchasing and equipping the first house was about £8,000, of which £7,000 had to be borrowed at interest. Decorations and cleaning were the work of volunteers from the cooperating churches and included the help of a Youth group. A long waiting-list remained after the first six ladies took up residence in September 1964. Since that time the project has become deeply embedded in the life of the local churches. A magnificent tribute to its success was the gift by an anonymous donor of a second house, which was opened in June 1967.

The Abbeyfield venture was made possible by vision and by the sharing, across denominational boundaries, of a great wealth of professional experience. The Roman Catholics already had an active Housing Association, but it is doubtful if any of the rest of us could have contemplated the venture alone. In retrospect, many can now see the rightness of the principles which underlie Carr-Gomm's achievement. Abbeyfield depends on the initiative and responsibility of the local community. In terms of Housing programmes its contribution is greater than is at first apparent, for the Abbeyfield tenant is frequently a person vacating property far too large for the needs of a single person. But we are inclined to regard the principles of dignity, independence and local responsibility as more important to the community in the long run than a small addition to the number of housing units. In their spacious bed-sitting rooms the Abbeyfield tenants have their own belongings about them and, for the services they receive—the care of a house-keeper and two hot meals a day around a 'family' table—they pay a moderate but economic rental. We are surprised that it has sometimes been necessary to explain that loneliness is not a peculiarity of persons dependent on the basic pension and social security, though Abbeyfield houses are designed with these as well as with others in mind. Carr-Gomm's principle of the open house has proved one of the most creative features of the venture; the houses are open to the comings and goings of neighbours and privacy is linked with abundant friendship. Inter-church rotas maintain services on the house-keeper's day off and the Ministerial Staff co-operate in providing monthly (united) Communion Services.

Abbeyfield Addiscombe is only part of the widespread development of the voluntary housing association in Croydon and throughout the country. It was a satisfaction to St. Mary Magdalene to be able to assist in the local Roman Catholic housing plans by making available a former clergy house. The Addiscombe Churches have been able to contribute personnel to the committee of the Croydon Council of Churches Housing Association, whose plans include the provision of at-cost accommodation for special classes of people, as, for instance, unsupported mothers (the first house was so allocated), newly married couples and the lonely elderly. The possible redeployment of unnecessarily large church premises has not been overlooked. In our immediate Parish are the forty-five cost-rent flats of the Bishop of Croydon's Birdhurst Housing Association, and local ministers, with others, have been able to recommend cases of need brought to their notice. The Housing Department of our local authority has welcomed the work of the voluntary associations[16] and recognised their particular value to those who, though in urgent need, cannot

[16] See also the Milner-Holland Report on London Housing, 1965.

be given priority over others in the 'points' system for the allocation of publicly owned housing.

A simple contribution to an allied need has been the recent opening of a 'Register of Surplus Furniture'. By this simple device we have been able to use one need to contribute to the solution of another. The one need is to obtain items of good, clean, second-hand furniture, where financial resources are severely limited; the other need (only too well known and recognisable) is means for second-hand furniture disposal. As a Group we have therefore appointed a secretary whose responsibility is to record details of available surplus furniture, its general description, dimensions and condition, and to note the date beyond which the owner is not willing to retain it. The alerting of the neighbourhood to the scheme has been through church and parish magazines. The remainder of the work is in the hands of the Guild of Social Service in association with the interested statutory workers. A telephone may be all that is necessary to ascertain whether some item is available in the Addiscombe area.

Our closest association with others has probably been in the broad and complex field covered by the Borough Welfare Services Department and by the Croydon Guild of Social Service.[17] The association of welfare officers with the other main departments which we have mentioned adds to the complexity, and we have increasingly appreciated the key position of the 'Guild' as the recognised liaison body between the statutory and voluntary services. The main, though not exclusive concern of the Welfare Services department, as such, is the care of the elderly and handicapped, and part of the Church's contribution has been through individuals giving their services to such voluntary organisations as the Voluntary Association for the Blind, the Hard of Hearing Club and the Darby and Joan Clubs. Both local authority and private

[17] See Addresses, page 164, National Council of Social Service.

homes for the elderly are included in the normal pattern of the Church's pastoral care, and a flexible 'division of labour' between the churches has been found helpful. We have already described the Saturday Services for the Elderly and Handicapped.[18] But our major concern for several years has been with the ageing, elderly or handicapped unable or unwilling to benefit from the many forms of provision which would bring them into the company of others. When the former County Borough of Croydon was reorganised on a 'social welfare' basis, following the National Assistance Act of 1948, the Borough was divided into seven areas, of which Addiscombe and Shirley was one. In this area the Welfare Department at the present time has a case-load of about 900, which includes the elderly, blind and physically handicapped. Within the elderly category, some are considered 'at risk'.[19] With the addition of further staff, the Department hopes to reduce the maximum period between routine visits by Welfare Officers to six months,[20] but the claims upon the neighbour-care of the professing Christian are self evident. We do not overlook the part played by loyal relatives (though they do not always exist), the doctor, nurse, home-help, insurance representative and the milkman, but, as our visiting has discovered, the gaps are large and deep.

An illustration of our involvement in the field of the Welfare Department is provided by Mr. N. A medical social worker in a local hospital asked if we could help a patient, shortly to be discharged, who had been offered a Council flat. Transport was required to take him successively from hospital to Housing Department, the flat, the Housing Department again, the Gas Board and back to Hospital. Eventually the (Methodist) Group Organiser found the (Anglican) driver, while, a few

[18] Chapter 5, page 72f.
[19] Minutes, Welfare Services Committee, 10 April 1967.
[20] *Ibid.*

days later, a lady (Roman Catholic) made available to Mr. N. her total furnishings prior to her own departure for an Old People's Home. A lady without active church association, who 'loved old people', offered to make a regular call. The day we were asked to help Mr. N. the Group Organiser had two further requests: one was from the Children's Case-work Department, asking if we could provide a child-minding service and occasional transport in an area of the Borough where no such help was discoverable; the other was from a local General Practitioner who informed us of the case of a difficult elderly person over whom the 'neighbours had gone on strike'. We were unable to help in the former case; we were able to mount a 'holding' operation in the latter.

Miss Cornwall has described something of the work of the Addiscombe Church's 'second-line' visitors.[21] The Guild of Social Service has been the invaluable advisor, helping us to direct limited man-power to the places where it is most needed. In November 1966 we held our first consultation under 'Guild' auspices. About forty church visitors (fewer than we had hoped, but including Methodist Class Leaders, Anglican Road Wardens and Roman Catholic members of the order of St. Vincent de Paul) were able to meet Miss Elizabeth Crawley, then general secretary of the Guild, together with the Senior Welfare Officer of the Addiscombe area and two Moral Welfare workers. The professional workers' generous appraisal of the Church's contribution was tempered by courteous counsel: helpers must know the available social services, they must know the next link in their organisation, they must know when they need help and where to turn for it, they must be totally 'non-judgemental', they must go as friends and they must be prepared to keep simple records.

During 1967, several of our workers were formally associated with the Guild's 'Adopter' scheme, whereby persons offering

[21] Chapter 4, page 57f.

friendship are asked to accept the discipline of a regular visit and a quarterly report. In January 1968, the Addiscombe Group of Churches was represented by eight workers at a gathering of 'Adopters' held at the Home Help Training Centre. A survey of the training and work of the statutory Home Help proved of lively and practical interest.

The Addiscombe/Shirley Laymen's conference of March 1968[22] to which reference has already been made, took consultation with statutory and voluntary workers a further stage. The conference created mutual trust and enabled us to envisage a much clearer structure of relationship. For the Shirley Group of Churches, it represented the moment of decision to organise its pastoral resources as a whole in the service of the whole community; for the Addiscombe Group it 'gave' us Naomi Williams as 'Welfare Liaison Officer' to work jointly with Dorothy Cornwall.

We confess that cooperation with others has not been an easy discipline for us. Some of our churches have a long tradition of lay pastoral care and individuals are reluctant to let it be known, even to their clergy or ministers, what they do. There is a deep sense that neighbourliness is essentially spontaneous and 'in secret',[23] requiring no complicated organisation, still less a trumpet. This Christian insight we deeply respect and we are confident that, in our cooperation with the Guild, we shall find a way of reconciling this sensitivity to the urgent claims of coordination. Relationship with the qualified case-worker is another sensitive area. We are well aware of the charge of amateurism and know that there are limits to the service we can offer. But the over-critical professional worker does not command our entire sympathy. Even human beings requiring the help of a skilled case-worker do not live in a vacuum between one visit and the next. When the specialist has gone home the neighbour is still there,

[22] Chapter 7, page 113ff. [23] Matt. 6: 2–6.

incapable by human feeling and physical proximity of remaining totally uninvolved. The policy of offering new housing units (particularly flat dwellings) to the most 'deserving' may sometimes overlook the daunting problem of good neighbourliness presented to the few active tenants.

At the Addiscombe/Shirley Conference on 'Christian Care and the Welfare Services', representatives were asked to say what they believed was 'distinctive' about 'Christian' neighbourliness. We found a quotation from *The Pastoral Ministry Today*, a pamphlet of the Clinical Theological Association,[24] more convincing than some other statements we have read of the distinctive Christian role:

'Society has organised its (own) pastors to meet the emotional needs and the social crises through the welfare services. We might at first sight want to differentiate these from the pastoral care of the Church . . . Yet immediately one is reminded that the marks of the Kingdom were precisely such acts . . . How does the Church work alongside these new pastors and what support is it prepared to offer them . . .?

'If we are to find any satisfactory answer . . . we will have to have a firm theological view of the nature of total pastoral care, both in its temporal aspects and in the ultimate aim of relating a person to God. For it is this latter which gives anything more than temporary meaning to the individual alleviations which are produced. Medical care can only heal a man of one disease in order that ultimately he may die of another. It does not hold the key of immortality . . . It is only when there is some sense of eternal purpose communicated through a particular situation that a person is growing towards a maturity which will help cope with the next crisis which will inevitably succeed the present one. It is this sense of ultimate meaning because a person is confronted with the love of God that is the specific ingredient in our Christian pastoral care.'

[24] See Addresses, p. 164.

7. In Conference

IN this chapter we provide some 'ready-made' material which we hope may be of use to others desiring to 'learn together'.[1] Since, in great measure, they prepared the way for the larger conference, we describe, first, the annual study conferences of the Addiscombe and Shirley Area Council of Churches, providing two examples of the material we used; we then turn to the more ambitious venture which attempted to bring together representatives from the churches of the whole London Borough of Croydon. As we hope to show, the two types of conference differed in more than geographical coverage and may represent two aspects of the joint study-conferences envisaged in the Nottingham report.

There were numerous anticipations of joint church study in Addiscombe. There were the Anglican-Methodist retreats of 1949[2]; from February 1st to 3rd, 1952 a united laymen's conference was held at the Addiscombe Methodist Church; in subsequent years, lecture series and Bible Weeks, held at St. Mildred's, were organised with a view to the participation of other churches. But it was not until 1963, the year of the publication of the *Anglican-Methodist Report*, that the study conferences became a permanent feature of the life of the Church. On a Saturday in the March of that year, about sixty-five representatives from ten churches met at St. Mildred's to study 'How our Churches came into being'. Papers were read by lay members of the Church of England, Baptist, Methodist and Presbyterian churches, the clergy and ministers being barred from the conference until 4.15 p.m. There was

[1] Nottingham resolution, Section 5, B 2. See Chapter 2, page 19.
[2] Chapter 3, page 30.

opportunity for group discussion and a final act of Worship. The duration of the conference on this first occasion was 10.45 a.m. to 6.30 p.m. and this involved the preparation of a mid-day meal; all subsequent conferences (partly from considerations of size) have been limited to the afternoon and early evening. It has not been easy to reconcile full diaries with the desire for unhurried time together and we know that the week-end retreat will have to find its place again within the pattern of our common Christian life.

The strictly 'lay' nature of the 1963 Conference was abandoned the following year when four ministers, Anglican, Baptist, Congregationalist and Methodist, formed a 'brains trust' on the scriptural basis of the Service of Holy Communion. Bible references and questions had already been prepared both for the ministers and for the lay representatives. In 1965, having felt rather over-loaded by four ministerial contributions, we returned to the lay principle, and in what was generally felt to be a more constructive conference, two laymen introduced the theme, 'Down to Earth', a study of the doctrine and experience of the Holy Spirit. 1965 was notable for its wide church representation: we had aimed at about 144 representatives drawn from twelve churches; in the event, 130 attended from thirteen churches. These included six Anglican, two Baptist, one Congregationalist, three Methodist and one Pentecostal 'New Testament Church of God in Christ'. The contribution of the (West Indian) Church of God was one of the most valuable experiences of this particular conference, which concluded with a united service of Holy Communion celebrated by the Bishop of Croydon.[3]

Up to this time, St. Mildred's, with its extensive premises, had provided the natural study centre, but in 1966 we moved to the only other premises in the area able to cope with twelve study groups, the Shirley Methodist. A study of the

[3] See Chapter 9, page 145.

New Testament Church according to the Acts of the Apostles had been clearly influenced by the Nottingham study sections. A local reporter wrote up the conference under the title, 'What Has Happened to the Explosive Force of the Church?' A valid criticism was that individual church groups seemed to remain segregated in the open sessions. We took note of this and the other criticisms. P.N.D.[4] was allowed to take precedence over the area study conference in 1967, but for 1968 we planned 'Christian Care and the Welfare Services', the theme almost forced upon us by the increasing commitments of the church visitors and our growing relationship with the trained welfare workers.

Before providing the outline of the 1965 and 1968 conferences, we should describe, briefly, the pattern of organisation. We have been fortunate in that the lay secretary of the Addiscombe and Shirley Area Council has been willing to act as organiser. With February–March as the established conference-time, the normal practice has been for the Council to agree the general theme in the previous June. A sub-committee, about four in number, has then formed itself into a work-party to draw up detailed plans for submission to the autumn meeting. It has thus been possible to send out preliminary notice, with conference outline, to all ministers and church secretaries at the beginning of November. To maintain continuity we have asked that half of the previous year's representatives be included in the ensuing conference. We have further asked that a proportion of representatives be under the age of thirty. The practice of including, for each church, a list of their previous representatives, has testified to the efficiency of our secretary, if not to that of the churches. Courteous reminders have still been necessary (to the present writers as to others) to obtain the names by the end of the year. Shortly afterwards, representatives have received their

[4] See Addresses and Abbreviations p. 164f.

personal note of welcome, the programme, study suggestions, identity disk and group number. The study conferences have increasingly been used as the basis of study—whether for inter-church or denominational groups—during the preceding months, and the ministerial staff have usually found it necessary to contribute suggestions for Bible study and other reading related to the conference theme.

We provide, then, two examples of study outlines, as they were despatched to the church representatives.

Example One

NAME:

CROYDON COUNCIL OF CHRISTIAN CHURCHES—
ADDISCOMBE/SHIRLEY AREA

Inter-church Lay Conference at St. Mildred's Church, Bingham Road, on Saturday, 20 February 1965. 2 p.m. to 7.30 p.m.

'Down to Earth'

The Teaching and Experience of the Holy Spirit

Dear Friend,

We are glad to know that you have been appointed a representative from your Church to the Conference. If unavoidably prevented from attending please inform the Secretary at once and undertake, if at all possible, to provide a substitute.

The Time-table is as follows:

2.00 p.m. Gathering
2.10 p.m. Introductions—Rev. E. N. Goodridge
2.15 p.m. Opening Devotions—Rev. M. Cooper
2.30 p.m. 'Down to Earth'—the theme is introduced by Mr. Robert C. Scotchmer and Mr. Jim Stone

IN CONFERENCE

3.15 p.m. Study Groups (the numbers at the foot of this note indicate your group and study section)
4.30 p.m. Tea
5.15 p.m. Open Session under the chairmanship of the Rev. Brian J. Galliers
6.30 p.m. Holy Communion Service in Church when all who are moved to do so are invited to participate. The Celebrant will be The Right Reverend the Lord Bishop of Croydon.
The Communion Service will commence with ten minutes silent meditation.

Please endeavour to make personal preparation for the Conference and remember to bring with you your Bible and material for note-taking. There will be a collection to meet the expenses.

Please write your name and church affiliation on the enclosed Identity Disk and bring it with you.

Sincerely yours,

Chairman
Secretary

Your group number:
Your study number:

MATERIAL FOR GROUP STUDY

STUDY 1   'The Spirit in the World'

Scripture:

Genesis 1:1–2.   At Creation
Exodus 31:1–5.   In human skill
Romans 2:11–16.   In the non-believer?

Honest to God:
Is the Holy Spirit at work in the world outside the Church? Give examples.

Down to Earth:
  What bearing does this have (if any) upon—
  1. your secular employment?
  2. the witness of the church?

STUDY 2 'The Spirit as the Life of His People'

Scripture:
  Ezekiel 37:1–14.   Resurrection of his people
  Zechariah 4:6.   Restoration of his people
  Acts 2:1–4.   Empowering of his people

Honest to God:
  'The faith of the Bible is faith in a God who raises the dead.' Illustrate further.

Down to Earth:
  What evidence (if any) do you find in the Church today that God works impossibilities? If not, why not?

STUDY 3 'The Spirit and the Birth of the New Life in the Individual Believer'

Scripture:
  Psalm 51:1–4 and 10–13.   Prayer of the penitent
  John 3:1–8.   Spiritual birth
  1 Peter 1:3.   Born again

Honest to God:
  What are the essential marks of the re-birth?

Down to Earth:
  'You've either got it or you haven't: there's nothing you can do about it.' Comment.

STUDY 4 'The Spirit and the Growth of the New Life in the Individual Believer.'

Scripture:
  Romans 8:14–17.   Sons of God

Galatians 5:22–25.   Spiritual Fruit
Colossians 3:12–15.   New garments

Honest to God:
What are the chief marks of a life which is being nourished by the Spirit?

Down to Earth:
Are these marks evident in the lives of Christians more than in others? If not, why not?

STUDY 5   'The Gifts of the Spirit to His Church'

Scripture:
  1 Corinthians 12:4–11 and 27–31.   Various gifts
  1 Corinthians 13.   The greatest gift
  1 Corinthians 14:1.   A great gift

Honest to God:
With what gifts does the Spirit endow the Church for its mission in the world?
In what order of importance are we to place them?

Down to Earth:
Which of these gifts appear to have departed from the life of the church?
Are any of these gifts to be found in new guises?
How far do you conclude the Church has become spiritually impoverished and why?

STUDY 6   'The Spirit in Preaching and Prophecy'
        'The Spirit as "guide into all the truth"'

Scripture:
  Acts 2:14–18.   Upon all flesh
  John 14:15–17; 25–26.   Spirit of truth
  John 16:7–14.   Spirit of conviction
  Matthew 10:19–20.   'In that hour'

Honest to God:
   What do these passages teach of the continuing work of the Holy Spirit in the Church?

Down to Earth:
   'Ye do always resist the Holy Ghost: as your fathers did so do ye' (Stephen). Is the Church any more ready to receive truth than its fore-runner, Israel?
   What sort of things do you believe the Spirit is saying to the Churches today?

NOTES:

It is expected that two groups will be studying each of the six sections outlined above.

The question entitled 'Honest to God' is intended to draw out the meaning of the Bible passages.

The question entitled 'Down to Earth' is intended to draw out practical implications and encourage a spirit of complete honesty.

Leaders are asked to keep their groups as far as possible to the matter in hand and not to stray into fields of study covered by other groups.

It is suggested that approximately half the time available should be spent on the Bible Study and half on the questions. Ten minutes should be allowed for quiet and prayer: this is all the more important if discussion reveals differences of understanding. 'God is not a God of confusion, but of peace.'

At the commencement of group study it will be helpful if in addition to wearing the identity disk each member gives his or her name, occupation and church affiliation.

Example Two

NAME:

CROYDON COUNCIL OF CHRISTIAN CHURCHES, ADDISCOMBE/
SHIRLEY AREA

ANNUAL LAY STUDY CONFERENCE

Saturday, 2nd March, 1968 at Shirley Methodist Church, Shirley Road. 2.30 p.m. to 7.30 p.m.

'Christian Care and the Welfare Services'

Dear Friend,

We are glad to know that you have been appointed a representative of your church to the Conference. If unavoidably prevented from attending, please inform your minister and the secretary and, if at all possible, provide a substitute.

Sincerely yours,

Chairman
Secretary

Timetable:

2.00 p.m.   Assemble
2.10   Introduction. Conference Chairman
2.15   Devotions
2.30   *Group Work* 1
Section A. (Groups 1—6) Biblical Study
            'Neighbour care in Law and Gospel'
Section B. (Groups 7—12) Social Study
            'Neighbour care through Church and
            "Welfare" '
2.30   *Open Session* 1
            Main and supplementary reports from groups
            (Section A.)

EXPERIMENT IN UNITY

        Main and supplementary reports from groups
        Comments by observers. Questions and
        Discussion.   (Section B.)

4.30   Tea

5.15   *Group Work 2*
        'What would you do?' Groups consider four 'cases'
        (w) Groups 1—3   (x) Groups 4—6
        (y) Groups 7—9   (z) Groups 10—12

6.15   *Open Session 2*
        Main and supplementary reports
        Comments by observers
        Towards some conclusions
        The Church's place. Our training and deployment

7.15   Act of Dedication

Our observers: Welcome to Mr. Ernest Tite, General Secretary of the Guild of Social Service, to Mr. H. P. Muller, Coordinator, Croydon Voluntary Aid Project and representative of the National Association of Mental Health, and to representatives of statutory and voluntary Welfare.

Your preparation: In addition to the Bible passages overleaf, we suggest the following reading: *Consumer's Guide to the British Social Services*, Pelican, and *Christians and Social Work* by Kathleen Heasman, S.C.M.

You are particularly asked to study the section in Groupwork 1 to which you have *not* been allocated. Bring Bible and notebook.

Please complete the identity disk with your name and affiliation and wear throughout the conference.

Please be prepared to share what you may have learnt in the conference with members of your own church or fellowship.

Conference Secretary: Miss Muriel King, 50 Compton Road, 654 3395
Your group number:
Your group leader:

MATERIAL FOR STUDY

'Christian Care and the Welfare Services'

Group Work 1 *Section A*   *Groups* 1—6
  Neighbour Care in Law and Gospel

a. *The Law*

    Leviticus 19:9–18; 33; 34. Love your neighbour
    Questions:
    Who is my neighbour according to the Levitical law?
    What did neighbourliness mean in practical terms?

b. *The Gospel*

    Luke 4:16–21   The Gospel programme.
    Matthew 5:43–48   Only your brothers?
    Luke 10:25–37   Who is my neighbour?
    Compare John 8:49 Samaritan devils.
    Questions:
    Who is my neighbour according to the Gospel?
    What does this neighbourliness mean in practical terms?

c. *The Law of the Gospel of Christ*

    Does Jesus make any distinction between neighbourliness towards one's own co-religionaries and neighbourliness towards others?
    Does the teaching and practice of Jesus justify making a distinction between the 'spiritual' and the 'material' need of one's neighbour?

What difference do you think there may be between the neighbourliness of a professing Christian and the neighbourliness of: 1. a non-church-going friend, 2. a visitor from a voluntary association—e.g. the Polio Fellowship, 3. a salaried officer of a Welfare Department?

What do you conclude is distinctive about Christian neighbourliness? How distinctive is it in practice?[1]

Group Work 1 Section B　　　　　　　　　　　*Groups 7—12*

Neighbour Care Through Church and 'Welfare' Agencies

a. *The Church*

Who is responsible for pastoral care in your church?
How does it work?
Who comes within it?
What does it do?

b. *Other Agencies*

What do you know of the work of other agencies of care?
What are they? Voluntary? Statutory?
Whom do they serve?
What do they do?

c. *The Church and Others*

What differences do you find between the two sorts of caring: 1. in objectives? 2. in 'clientele? 3. in the service rendered?

Do your answers disturb or satisfy you? Either way, say why.
What do you find in common between the two sorts of caring?
Do you find any grounds for believing that the two might cooperate?

What do you conclude is distinctive about Christian neighbourliness? How distinctive is it in practice?[2]

[1,2] This is where the two sections of work converge.

It will be noted that in 'Group Work 2' the members of the above conference were asked to consider four case histories. These were compiled in consultation with the representative of the National Association for Mental Health, the senior case-worker of the Guild of Social Service, a retired industrial welfare officer (a member of our committee) and our own Addiscombe Group Organiser. Since even disguised or imaginary cases cannot help but bear resemblance to known persons, we only provided this material for the previous study of group leaders and do not print it here. The aim was to present a fairly typical human situation, not so much as the trained social worker might describe it, but as it might be observed by the ordinary church worker or neighbour. We then relied on the professional (we tried to have someone with case-work experience in each group) to indicate where the complexities might lie and to guide the church worker in obtaining the appropriate help. In submitting six confidential (though disguised) case histories to us, a professional case-worker indicated that, 'in all these cases professional help was necessary, but . . . the voluntary worker has an important part to play, sometimes in recognising the need for help . . . and later in providing friendship and care . . .'

As we have indicated, the 'all-Croydon' conference was a more ambitious project and had in mind a different objective. The initiative came from the Executive Committee of the Croydon Council of Christian Churches—a body which we see much as the servant of the numerous area or group councils within the Borough. Believing that Nottingham 1964 was a matter for local discovery rather than for top-level direction, the Executive, with the support of the full Council, appointed a working-party to explore the possibilities of a residential conference for the churches of the London Borough of Croydon. Numerous difficulties were noted: the 'different positions' reached in different areas of the Borough, the 'different levels of understanding and interest' and, not least, the 'variety of courses and schemes to which the churches of different traditions are committed or summoned'. Those of us responsible for the later stages of the conference were to discover, too, an element (almost) of hostility to this new entity called the 'London Borough of Croydon' in which the Church now found itself. However, the working-party believed 'that the value of such a conference would be the opportunity it would provide for Christian people to meet one another' and recommended a week-end in 1966. In March 1965 a letter was accordingly sent to all churches having some association with the central Council. There was little response. With exemplary faith, the Rev. E. C. Urwin, our veteran ecumenical leader, pressed on with a preparatory study-booklet, *Mission, Unity and the Local Church*[5] and this was used widely in the Borough during the winter 1965–6. In November a new working-party took over the organisation, abandoned the plan for a residential conference and arranged instead for a gathering in the superb new premises of the George Street Congregational Church, Addiscombe Grove.

In November 1965 we despatched an introductory letter, inviting the names of two representatives or one "contact", to about 140 church bodies. It seemed ironical that the list of such bodies had to be obtained from the Public Library and then carefully checked and corrected in order that the Croydon Council of Christian Churches might know, precisely, whom it existed in principle to represent. Further communications were necessary in February and March 1966, to encourage the uncommunicative, welcome the responsive and provide up-to-date information for the interested. When the conference took place at the end of April, forty-nine churches were represented, all by two or more of their people. They included:

[5] A few surplus copies are available from the Group Secretary, 50 Compton Road, Croydon.

twenty-two Anglican, nine Methodist, five Baptist, five Congregationalist, two Society of Friends, and one each of Brethren, 'Liberal Catholic', Presbyterian, Roman Catholic, Salvation Army and Unitarian. The last had been omitted from our original invitations but asked if they might be permitted to come; their presence was most valuable, especially in the groups on which they served. The presence of six Roman Catholic members made it possible for the majority of the ten study groups to have a Roman Catholic member—another of many memorable features of this conference. It will be noticed that we dispensed entirely with formal addresses, making it possible for the groups (covering six fields of study) to engage in three work-sessions before the final, plenary session. The whole conference was indebted to the Bishop of Croydon, the Right Rev. John T. Hughes, for the way in which he led prayer and meditation throughout; this more than all else gave to the whole experience a transcending quality.

Example Three

THE NEW LONDON BOROUGH OF CROYDON
ECUMENICAL STUDY CONFERENCE 29–30 APRIL 1966.

Organised by the Croydon Council of Christian Churches
Theme: 'Mission, Unity and the Local Church'

George Street Congregational Church, Addiscombe Grove, Friday 7.0 p.m. to Saturday 4.30 p.m.

TIME TABLE

Friday

7.00 p.m.   Registration and Gathering in Church

EXPERIMENT IN UNITY

7.30 p.m.	Devotions and Introduction. The Bishop of Croydon The Right Rev. John T. Hughes, M.A.
8.00 p.m. to 9.00 p.m.	GROUP STUDY SESSION 1
9.00 p.m. to 9.20 p.m.	Refreshments
9.20 p.m.	Evening Prayers

Saturday

9.30 a.m.	Assembling (Registration for those unable to come on Friday)
10.00 a.m.	Devotions in Church. Announcements
10.15 to 11.15 a.m.	GROUP STUDY SESSION 2
11.15 to 11.45 a.m.	Coffee Break
11.45 to 12.45 p.m.	GROUP STUDY SESSION 3
1.00 p.m.	Lunch in Hall
2.30 p.m.	Group reports OPEN SESSION Consideration of any recommendations or resolutions
4.00 p.m.	Closing Worship
4.15 p.m.	Light Refreshments

GROUP-STUDIES

Introduction

The Group studies are based on the booklet prepared for the Croydon Council of Christian Churches by the Rev. E. C. Urwin. In the following notes prepared for Conference representatives, additional Bible references are provided and the questions selected and re-shaped to meet the needs of the three Study-sessions. It will obviously not be possible for all the Biblical material to be considered in groups, but it is hoped you will use it in your preparation.

IN CONFERENCE 121

The pattern of study is similar for all groups, though only one or two will be studying the same material. In session 1. each group considers the Biblical evidence; in session 2. the group looks at the situation as we find it; in session 3. the group is required to bring the Biblical insights to bear upon the situation. The three sessions are given the titles:

'The Bible' 1.
'The World' 2.
and 'The Church' 3.

It is hoped that each study session will commence with prayer, silent or spoken, and that there will be at all times a consciousness of the Holy Spirit 'who will lead you into all the truth'. The 'open' session on the Saturday afternoon should be looked upon as a time when your leader (or appointed spokesman) briefly summarises the ground you have covered and shares with the whole Conference any deep concerns or convictions which may have arisen.

Notes: In the following Study material 'Nottingham' refers to the Report from the first British Conference on Faith and Order, Nottingham 1964, 'Unity Begins at Home' (S.C.M., 3/6). 'E. C. Urwin' refers to the duplicated Study outline provided.

THE NEW LONDON BOROUGH OF CROYDON
ECUMENICAL STUDY CONFERENCE APRIL 29th to 30th, 1966
'Mission, Unity and the Local Church'

MATERIAL FOR GROUP STUDY:

STUDY 1. 'World Church'   Leader
                              Group(s)

Session One—The Bible

What sense of a 'world' Church do you find in the New Testament? In its mission? Life? Organisation?

In addition to E. C. Urwin references see: Rom. 1:8–16 ('Throughout the whole world'); Rom. 15:18–29 ('Spain')
Do you find any evidence of cleavages (theological, ecclesiastical), in the New Testament Church?
(See Paul ad lib. espec. Gal. 2:11–13. ('I resisted him'); 1 Cor. 1:10–13 ('contentions'); 2 Cor. 11:1–6 ('a different gospel'); Phil. 1:12–18 (proclaiming 'Christ of faction').

Session Two—The World

What do you know of the processes which led to the formation of the World Council of Christian Churches and its constituent national bodies?
What evidence do you find that this is a movement of the Holy Spirit?
What do you know of the so-called 'International Council of Christian Churches', which is opposing the work of the World Council?
See 'Nottingham', pages 7–14, 35–37, etc.

Session Three—The Church

What picture of a 'World' Church have you received? What attitude do you believe is required of you towards professing Christians whose understanding, being different from your own, may lead them to ascribe to man (or to the devil) that which you believe to be of God? How do you believe we should set about creating a true image of the 'world' Church at local level?

STUDY 2.   'The Church in Croydon'   Leader
                                     Group(s)

Session One—The Bible

What does the New Testament teach of divisions, distinctions and groupings in the life of the Church?

IN CONFERENCE

In addition to E. C. Urwin see: Gal. 2:1–10 ('I resisted him'); 1 Cor. 3:1–9 (Paul and Apollos); 1 Cor. 12:4 onwards ('diversities of gifts'); Rom. 14:1 onwards (eating customs); John 15:1 onwards (The Vine)

What are the basic New Testament convictions about the Church's unity? In its Mission? Its Life? Its structure?

Session Two—The World

What do you know of inter-church relationships in Croydon? (A special summary will be available to the group)
What do you believe would have been the judgement of the Apostle Paul on this situation?

Session Three—The Church

In what ways do you believe the churches in Croydon might become, more evidently, the 'Church in Croydon'? Is there anything you would wish to say to the 140 congregations in the Borough?
See 'Nottingham', pages 43–48 and Section 5B, pages 78–79

STUDY 3. 'Our Faith'   Leader
                       Group(s)

Session One—The Bible

What does the New Testament teach are the fundamental elements of the Christian Faith? In doctrine, experience, life? In addition to E. C. Urwin, which concentrates on the Church, you may wish to look up: Acts 13:16–41 (The early Preaching); 1 Cor. 15:1–11 (The Tradition); 1 Cor. 1:17–18 (The Word of the Cross); Rom. 1:1–17 (The Gospel of Christ); Gal. 3:1–9 (Faith).
See 'Nottingham', pages 58–59

Session Two—The World

Can you illustrate from the New Testament ways in which different modes of thought are employed to interpret the Person and Work of Christ to different people? Does the sower have to consider the soil in which he is sowing?
See 1 Cor. 9:18–22 (All things to all men); Rom. 2:11–16 (Jew and Gentile considered); Gal. 4:21–31 (the Gospel illustrated for the Jew); Eph. 2:11–3:11 (the Gospel illustrated for the Gentile). You may find it helpful to consider different New Testament interpretations of the cross (e.g. sacrifice, justice, love, victory).

Session Three—The Church

In what ways may the Gospel be communicated to men and women today in terms that they can understand, without comprising its unchanging validity? To what extent do you believe the Gospel requires a language of its own? To what extent do you believe certain standards of belief to be a pre-requisite of united witness?
See 'Nottingham', pages 28–32 and 38 and 75.

STUDY 4. 'Our Worship and Ministry'
                                        Leader
                                        Group(s)

Session One—The Bible

What sources of Christian Worship do you find in the Bible? The Temple? The Synagogue? The Upper Room? Is there anything to be learnt about Worship from the Old Testament? Priesthood? (consider Moses and Aaron). What elements do you conclude are fundamental to Christian Worship?
See N.T. references; E. C. Urwin.

IN CONFERENCE

Session Two—The World

What traditions of Christian Worship are represented in your group? Is each member convinced of the adequacy of the Worship with which he is familiar, or is there any sense of 'something missing'? With what 'experiments' and developments in Worship are you aware?

See 'Nottingham', pages 61–64; Section 2, page 76.

Session Three—The Church

(Group 4A)

What diversity of Worship do you envisage in a 'united' Church and what relationship do you conceive might be possible between one tradition and another? Do you think a universally recognised Ministry would help here?

(Group 4B)

Consider the functions of 'Ministry' implied in such words as: Apostle, Prophet, Teacher (1 Cor. 12:28): Evangelist, Pastor/Shepherd (Eph. 4:11); Steward (Matt. 20:8); Deacon (Acts 6:3, Phil. 1:1); Elder (Acts 14:23); Bishop (Phil. 1:1); Servant/Minister (1 Cor. 12:5, etc.)

How are these ministries exercised in your Church? Can you imagine a pattern of Ministry which could be accepted by all Christians?

See 'Nottingham', pages 51–52; pages 67–71 and 77.

STUDY 5. 'Our Work among Children and Youth'

                              Leader
                              Group(s)

Session One—The Bible

What teaching do you find in the Bible concerning the responsibility and relationship of parents and Church to children and young people?

In addition to E. C. Urwin, see Exod. 20:12 (The Commandment); Deut. 6:4–7 (Teaching of the Commandments); Deut. 21:18–21 (Punishment of rebellion); Mal. 1:6 (parental reward). Key-word: Rebellion?

What other insights do you find regarding youth and son-ship?

In addition to E. C. Urwin, see Gen. 4:1–8 (A brother's murder); Isa. 1:2–4 (rebellious children); Hos. 11:1–9 (the longsuffering of love); Matt. 21:28–31 (Children want to conform); Luke 15:11–32 (the lost son); Gal. 3:23–4, 7 (childhood and adulthood); Rom. 8:12–19 (the revealing of the Sons of God). Key-word: Freedom?

Session Two—The World

What work among children and youth takes place in your own church?

What do you suppose its objects to be? How do these differ (if at all) from those of the Public Education and Youth Authority?

Session Three—The Church

Where do you believe the Church's work among children and young people is 'succeeding'? 'failing'? Has Church dis-unity anything to do with the failure? What convictions and patterns would you like to see re-shaping the Church's work with the new generation?

See 'Nottingham', Section 3, 1, 2, page 77; Section 5, B2, pages 78–9.

STUDY 6. 'The Church in the World'

                                Leader

                                Group(s)

Session One—The Bible

What meanings are given to the term 'the world' in the Bible?

What is the Christian attitude to the world?
In addition to E. C. Urwin, see your Concordance and Romans 2:11–16 (conscience outside faith).

Session Two—The World

What 'worldly' habits and activities do members of your group regard as 'out' for the professing Christian? How far are your judgements based upon fundamental Christian insights and how far upon a social or religious tradition? What evidence do you see in the world around you *a.* of the 'power of darkness' (Luke 22:53) and *b.* of the Activity of God?

'I pray not that thou shouldst take them out of the world.' Where in the world and how in the world does a Christian fulfil his ministry?

See E. C. Urwin, Study material and Questions.

See 'Nottingham', pages 51, 71–74 and Section 5B, pages 78–79.

The Croydon Conference felt bound to issue a statement addressed to all Christian bodies in the Borough. We testified to the deep sense of unity of which we had been conscious and asked that, as a Borough, we might be regarded as an 'area of ecumenical experiment'.[6] A surprising request was that conference *at this level* should become a permanent feature of the Church life of the Borough.[7] The Bishop of Croydon remarked that 'Christ had his three as well as his twelve'. We already knew the value of the group or area conferences, which, over the years, would enable a significant proportion of our congregations to do some 'learning together'; we had now found the value of a conference which

[6] Nottingham Resolutions, Section 5, B 3. See Chapter 2, p. 19.

[7] The Second all-Croydon Conference, on the theme 'The Spirit of Truth', took place in March 1968, sixty-five churches participating.

could bring together from a large urban area the top-level leadership of the churches. We found that we had far more to learn from each other than we had ever guessed and that we could no longer ignore the fact that, within the confines of a great London Borough, whether we liked it or not, we were the Church. The net result of the Croydon 'Nottingham' was to provide us with our agenda for many years to come: high on the agenda was our ministerial and lay colleagueship and the 'structuring' which would be necessary to express our new-found sense of mission and unity.

8. In Colleagueship

A layman who has long been associated with inter-church relationships in Addiscombe commented that, in writing of our experiment in unity we should find it difficult to assess the 'personal' factor. His reference was to the personal gifts of a succession of ministers of different denominations and to the notable colleagueship of certain of them. We have already[1] referred to the close association of the ministers of St. Mildred's and Addiscombe Methodist in the immediate post-war years and those in a better position to judge than ourselves see this particular colleagueship as probably the most significant factor in the earlier period of ecumenical development. Twenty years later, we would only venture the judgement that the close friendship of two ministers could not have had an abiding significance for the life of the Church in Addiscombe apart from a willingness for friendship at congregational level. Our own colleagueship was quickly recognised by our people and has no doubt made its own contribution to the sense of unity; at the same time we know that to some—whether justified or not—the impression has been given that 'phone conversations between ministers have 'settled' matters of some importance without adequate lay consultation.

For better or worse, ministerial relationships are of critical importance to the churches' discovery of themselves as Christ's Church in each place. In Addiscombe, as throughout the country, the Ministers' Fraternal has played an important part in fostering and maintaining this relationship through successive changes of personnel. Since the second World War the pattern has been a fluid one, formerly a gathering of

[1] Chapter 1, page 12.

ministers in the Addiscombe area alone, latterly a coming-together of ministers from the two areas of Addiscombe and Shirley. The Addiscombe Ministers' Staff meeting, which we describe later, is the most recent but a distinct development. At times, the Fraternal has been held together by the most tenuous of links—the subject of an occasional resurrection by a conscientious colleague. Yet it has been of immense value. There were the occasional days together in the countryside; there was the time when the group was joined by Father McKenna of the Church of Our Lady and by Father Leech of St. Luke's; there were the discussions and prayers, the silences and the confessions; and there was the blunt question asked of the Addiscombe Ministers by a senior colleague: 'What's your job anyway?' It was that question which settled for us whether or not we could 'spare the time' to meet every two months to work together at those visitation records.

For at least three of us in the Addiscombe Group of Churches, ministerial colleagueship has been influenced by participation in joint clergy and lay groups of Dr. Frank Lake's Clinical Theological Association,[2] described as a 'pioneering work on the frontier between theology and psychology'. The group to which two of us belonged for the two years 1965-66, was composed of about nine ministers (Anglican, Baptist, Congregational and Methodist) together with three women welfare workers—all Anglican. Ministerial expectations, in the main, were that the group might provide one with the equipment to deal less ineffectively with the problems of the mentally and emotionally distressed. After two years, we had learned, possibly, to be better listeners, and we had faced, too, deep areas of need where we knew that it was not within our competence to 'dispense' help in the way in which we once supposed we could. *Clinical Theology* proved its worth to us, not so much in our 'helping' of others

[2] See Addresses, page 164.

as in our coming to terms with ourselves. It was here that, playing the rôle of counsellor, we had to bear the humiliation of appearing to our colleagues ridiculous or incompetent. It was here that we began to recognise in ourselves—in our uneasy attitudes towards each other, our anxiety to relate the story reflecting credit on our own ministry, or our exaggerated notions of the scholarliness, vitality and 'success' of the other—the very symptoms of mental and emotional disturbance which we were being taught to recognise in others. The freedom with which, at length, we were able to examine the basic 'drives' of our own ministry, and, not least, the cost of them to wife and family, brought us to a much more honest relationship with each other, and (in all reverence) with God.

We do not claim that ministerial colleagueship must needs take root within the context of psychological study, but we think that those who have known *Clinical Theology* would tend to the judgement that some of its insights and all of its honesty are indispensable to the reconciliation of Christ's ministers to one another. We ask ourselves how far an 'unreconciled' ministry can effectively offer reconciliation to others. We must also ask what a 'Service of Reconciliation' can mean divorced from the practicalities of serious and honest colleagueship.

The development of the Addiscombe Ministerial Staff meeting took place alongside the wider Fraternal.[3] A Congregationalist minister, attending as an observer, said that it struck him as 'American' and left him unimpressed. He was looking for a 'fraternal' and had found, instead, a very busy 'staff'. The fact is that something had to be done to handle the pastoral material which began to flow steadily in after Dorothy Cornwall took over the organisation of the Home Mission. Sometimes two hours would be spent working together over the information and seeking the appropriate allocation of

[3] See also Chapter 4, page 54ff.

pastoral responsibility. But inevitably the field began to widen. Follow-up involved contacts with churches and organisations other than our own; publicity material needed constant revision in the light of experience and local circumstances; there were joint communications to church workers to be agreed and road-warden networks to be made or mended. When, at the beginning of 1967, the Addiscombe Group of Churches began to work as a distinct 'council'—though still retaining the former link with Shirley—the Ministerial Staff had their homework to do on the Group Council agenda. Miss Cornwall, who simply found herself the staff secretary, described us at an interim stage in our development: 'The Ministerial Staff of the Addiscombe Group are the clergy and ministers of seven of the churches, four of which are Anglican, two Methodist and one Roman Catholic. There are four more churches of other denominations in the Group, which do not yet wish to be associated with the project, although they are interested and like to be kept informed of developments.

'The Ministerial Staff meet in order to consider their joint activities. Meetings are held at the Catholic Presbytery. They are informal and no chairman having been appointed, one of the Staff exercises light control over the meeting. I act as their secretary and call them together. At first a brief calling notice sufficed but that has been replaced within twelve months by a more formal notice of agenda, containing anything from six to twelve items. I try to avoid paper work—no one has time for unnecessary reading—but the organisation is extending and when the Ministerial Staff make decisions which concern their respective churches, and which are to be referred to them, it is helpful to give the Staff a brief minute of the proceedings immediately after the meeting.'

Though we have called ourselves a 'staff', not a 'fraternal', we have grown in friendship as we have worked together and the consciousness of our common Christian calling, however differently interpreted, has been manifest. One of our most difficult experiences arose from the problem of working boundaries. Addiscombe is not a precisely defined area (except as an electoral ward) and for various reasons it was not unnatural that St. Luke's, Woodside, should link up with the Addiscombe Group of Churches. However, the nearby Congregationalist Church in Enmore Road, with many of its people drawn from St. Luke's Parish, has for long been associated with the South Norwood Council of Churches. The anomaly of two churches in the same area looking in opposite directions for inter-church fellowship became a temporary crisis as we began distributing the 'fish' signs bearing the legend: 'The Addiscombe Group of Churches'.[4] Unhappily, it was not simply a matter of agreeing boundaries: two adjacent churches, holding widely divergent views of the Church and Ministry, were faced with the problem of recognising each other's existence and of finding a way—at least—to coordinate two separately planned road-warden structures. A complex and delicate problem was solved in part by a change of wording: 'Addiscombe' was dropped and the window signs were made to read: 'The Local Group of Churches'. This, it seems, will be the necessary form of words in numerous 'boundary' situations. But the beginning of the deeper solution was the establishment of a working relationship between two ministers of different age, experience and church tradition, around the table at a Staff Meeting.

A matter of some concern to the present writers has been that of colleagueship with 'part-time' ministers. This arose in relation to a former pastor of a small Baptist Church in Morland Road (now known as the Addiscombe Baptist Church) as well as in our friendship with the leaders of the West Indian 'Church of God'.[5] The Baptist minister, whom we understood had been ordained, was largely debarred from

[4] See Chapter 4, page 61.   [5] See Chapter 2, page 21.

fellowship, even with his Baptist colleagues, by the necessity of a full-time secular job. Such friendship as one of us was able to offer was deeply appreciated.

Those of ministerial rank within the 'Church of God' are numerous. We have been introduced, at various times, to Bishops, Elders, Evangelists and Pastors. Apart from the question of 'orders', full-time secular occupation has again made it difficult for us to offer the fellowship we would have desired. The value set upon such fellowship was illustrated in June 1967, when Ernest wrote in the Methodist News-letter of some of the teachings associated with the Pentecostal movement. Hurt was caused, we feel, not so much by the querying of some allegedly 'biblical' teaching, as by the appearance of a break in fellowship. An hour of discussion between the Pentecostal leaders, Ernest and an experienced Methodist Local Preacher, may not have removed the theological problems but it certainly restored a warm Christian affection. We tentatively suggest that, as it becomes more customary for Ministers, Methodist Preachers and Anglican Readers to meet together, thought might be given to the offering of fellowship to one or another of the part-time ministers of smaller churches; we have known such men who would be open to the invitation and who would have their own valuable contribution to make.

As ministerial colleagueship has matured, so has the colleagueship of the lay fraternity. Service in voluntary agencies has played an important part: Free Church women have formed a team in the service of certain Old People's Homes, choir members of different churches join to help in local hospital services of worship, and likewise, in Prison after-care, Marriage Guidance, the Samaritans, Old People's Welfare, St. John Ambulance and in dozens of other ways, members of different congregations have become colleagues and friends. Colleagueship in the same daily profession, in an area from which so many are daily making their way to the

City, to similar offices and by the same trains, has also had its influence on the local church. The Home Fellowships have revealed some interesting encounters, as when conversation in a railway compartment led to a member of the Addiscombe Roman Catholic Church inviting to 'his' Home Fellowship a member of the Baptist Church at Woodside. The invitation was accepted.

The local Council of Churches is now a familiar part of the ecclesiastical scene in all parts of the country. Here it is that, within the limits set by local circumstances, ministers and laity of local churches are able to learn of each other, consult and cooperate. We give some account of our own Council of Churches only in so far as it illustrates two aspects of Christian colleagueship: the discovery of the appropriate 'unit of working' and the emergence of the ecumenical officer—or, as we would prefer to describe it, the servant of the whole Church.

Ernest has elsewhere described something of the rather intricate pattern of inter-church relationships within the London Borough of Croydon.[6] Within such a zone, ecumenical work is largely focussed upon small groups of churches, three to twelve in number, usually found within a natural geographical area, but associated for many other reasons, some recognised, some now almost forgotten. About twelve such groupings (usually working through an 'area council') exist in Croydon, and include about eighty-five out of a total of perhaps 140 recognisable Christian bodies. It is undoubtedly in this small, accepted grouping, that the real business of ecumenical encounter takes place. Yet we feel that the point might be taken too easily. We are not satisfied that sufficient thought is given to what we have called 'the appropriate unit of working'. It has been a disturbing experience to discover within ecumenical structures the same unquestioning urge to

[6] *The Church in the World*, Autumn 1966. B.C.C.

perpetuate one's own organisation as that which, in our innocence, we believed ecumenism had left behind.

Richard Taylor has invited the 'new Christian' to raise his eyes from a parochial level, recognising the various 'zones' in which people nowadays actually work and live. He asks how the Church 'can get off the fixed structures it now sits on, like Canute before the advancing tide, and become the missionary movement within the ebb and flow of today's situation'.[7] Without being entirely enamoured by his picture of 'a substantial regional structure . . . for the whole of metropolitan London . . . serving a variety of sub-zones' we do not deny the existence of Greater London (any more than the U.K. or the U.N.) as a major unit of the Church's operation. The experimental youth and community centre in Thornton Heath arises from sociological study and policy-thinking in terms of the whole metropolitan area.[8] We agree that a primary function of the Council of Churches is to relate the smaller group to the larger, so long as the recognition of the larger unit can be shown to have a clear 'word' to the Church in its local situation.

However, in a single London Borough (one of Taylor's 'sub-zones') we find ourselves struggling with a unit too big and diverse for us properly to comprehend. That we have to comprehend it and be the Church within it is something we have tried to recognise in the all-Croydon conferences. It was here that we gained first-hand knowledge of what was happening in other parts of the Borough and realised the urgent need for some means of continuing communication. It was evident that almost all areas had some particular experience to share and that there could be nothing but benefit from a generous recognition of the initiative taken by the other—say, in the field of housing, leadership training, evangelism or

[7] *New Christian*, 29 December 1966 and 12 January 1967.
[8] See Chapter 6, pages 92–3.

research into the possibilities of a Croydon Churches' Newspaper. The strange apprehension, in some quarters, of the work of a central Council of Churches, seems to derive from a total misconception of its function within the life of the whole Church. As the servant of the whole Church in one place (not the Directorship) we see it relating one part to another, encouraging the interest and support of all in the significant venture of the few, alerting the Church to new factors in the situation in which it finds itself and (as far as it is humanly possible) representing the whole Church to the whole community. The indefatigable labours of our Croydon Council secretaries are already bearing fruit in an increasing awareness of each other across the necessary working boundaries.

At the level of the 'area' group of churches, we have similarly had to learn of each other, recognise (and accept) the initiative of others and, in a changing situation, discover the appropriate units of operation. The task of discovery has been a confusing one, even for our most experienced leaders, and as ministers it is evident that we could have been more successful in communication. There was a period when church leaders confessed that they were obeying summonses to attend this and that meeting (it seemed to have a different title each time) without any clear picture of what it was about. The development is simple to see in retrospect. During 1964–5 St. Mary Magdalene and Addiscombe Methodist found it necessary to devise means of consultation at the highest level. The result was the calling of several joint Parochial Church Councils and Leaders' Meetings. While the joint body had no constitutional standing, it undoubtedly increased the sense of colleagueship and prepared our minds for the commitment to work together. Numerous engagements took place at committee level, particularly between the Sunday School staffs. But, as we have indicated elsewhere[9] our agenda could

[9] See Chapter 3, page 42f.

not be confined to the concerns of one parish. Thus, during 1966 it was felt wise to replace the 'PCC/LM' with a 'consultative group', involving a larger number of churches, each of which could be represented by minister and two or three laymen. Confusing as the change of policy may have been, it was this body which helped to establish the Home Fellowships and the Home Visiting as activities necessarily extending far beyond the bounds of one Anglican parish. As we have seen, apart from the cooperation of St. Mildred's, St. Luke's and the Addiscombe Roman Catholic Church, the Home Visiting, with its (now) tremendous significance for the life of the Church in our area, would in all probability never have survived.

The natural outcome of the 1966 Consultative Group was the creation, in 1967, of the distinct Addiscombe Group Council, with its growing agenda covering almost every aspect of the life and witness of the churches in the neighbourhood. The retention of a link with the Shirley area left a slightly confusing element in the situation but was both charitable and realistic. Shirley, with its more limited possibilities of church cooperation (comprising three Anglican churches and one Methodist) looked to us as a strengthening factor in its own development, while we valued the link with a different sociological area rich in people of experience and potential. The annual conferences continue as a 'twin-group' activity and illustrate the wisdom of a flexible structure.

Miss Cornwall describes for us the manner in which the new Addiscombe Group Council was enabled to open its joint Bank account! 'A group of churches working together in this way must have some sort of joint capital, and here we have been singularly fortunate . . . A sum of £100, bequeathed to one of the Church helpers by a lonely man whom she had visited for six months before he died, was handed over to the Addiscombe Group Council. It was used to provide a variety of stationery with the striking "fish" sign in black and white. The stationery included all-purpose quarto and foolscap duplicating paper, correspondence paper for the officers of the Group and visiting cards for the workers. Our bequest also provided the twelve-inch by six-inch "Sign of the Fish" cards for window display,[10] together with the comprehensive files of information for road wardens. After lavish expenditure it became obvious that something must be done to replace the initial capital. The churches represented on the Ministerial Staff were therefore asked to make voluntary contributions, varying from five to ten pounds according to means. With an income of about fifty pounds per annum we are hoping to be carried forward for another year, after which time we shall be able to see more clearly what cost is likely to be involved.'

Ministerial Staff Meeting and Group Council have 'thrown up' among us, lay men and women who, in a special sense, are the servants of the whole Church. We have mentioned the work of Miss Muriel King, in connection with the Study Conferences. Her work, as senior 'civil servant' of the Christian Ministry in the Addiscombe and Shirley areas, has held together the fabric of inter-church relationships for many years. Competently maintained records and a realistic assessment of ministerial office-efficiency are not the least of her contributions. The pre-occupation of individual churches with the urgent demands of their own life (and livelihood) could have severed, for months and even years, the ties that link them to one another, but for the diligence of a dedicated person willing to be the servant of the whole Church.

The Group Secretary (who is now serving both the Addiscombe and the Shirley areas) was eventually joined by the Group (Welfare) Organiser and much of our story revolves around her work.[11] Miss Cornwall's secretaryship of the

[10] Samples are available from the M. G. Press Ltd., 1–2 West Street, Croydon.
[11] See Chapter 4, pages 54–60 and Chapter 6, pages 88ff.

Ministerial Staff Meeting, her organisation of the House Visiting, her development of the inter-church Road Warden net-work, and her (almost unsought) liaison between the Church and the statutory and voluntary welfare authorities, have given us, as a Group of Churches, a new and unexpected concept of the place of the professional lay worker in colleagueship with the ministerial staff. (Miss Cornwall's full-time service has been unsalaried.) The realistic assessment of staff needs in the Addiscombe area cannot, in the future, ignore the work and the place of the lay Group Organiser.

Other ecumenical servants—as the Christian Aid Organiser and the recently appointed Home Fellowship officer—are at work among us, and their place in the life of the Church-in-Unity raises the question, so much alive in Anglican and Roman Catholic circles, of the place and function of the Diaconate. In the light of the work we have described we might think of the new Diaconate thus: 'The Diaconate shall be composed of Christian men and women, who, by virtue of particular qualifications, for example, in finance, administration, education, youth and community development, sociology, mental health, etc., are recognised and ordained by the Church as servants of the Church in the service of the world.' While this definition has in mind a close link with the Ministerial Staff of the Church, it does not necessarily conflict with the contention of W. J. Kilpatrick that the new Diaconate must be 'situational'—that is, related to a particular setting of need outside the accepted Church structure. We would agree with his picture of an order 'free to respond to new needs . . . counselling, hospital administration . . . teaching'. His suggestion that the Diaconate might include those able to 'devote one whole day a week to the voluntary service of those in need'[12] would in our situation, as in many others, include

[12] *New Christian*, 29 June 1967.

scores of men and women in our churches who are doing just this.

Our interest in a colleagueship which goes over the old parish boundaries does not persuade us that the typical Anglican urban parish has had its day. In Addiscombe we have found it an important unit of working and have further sub-divided it into manageable pastoral areas. It is within the parish context, where two or three contiguous churches are covenanted together to promote unity, that we can see most clearly a natural evolution of existing church structures to meet new needs. In *Parishes with a Purpose* Neville has written: 'the basic form of the local church in the parish has the potential for that kind of adaptation and development which is going to be demanded . . . either ecumenically or sociologically . . .'[13]

The 1967 Methodist Conference received a report on the streamlining of Methodist organisation. While it was not felt wise to make revolutionary changes while negotiations were still proceeding with the Anglican Church, changes were seen as necessary 'reformation'. Since these recommendations relate Methodism more closely, in certain respects, to the structures both of Anglicanism and of 'Independency', it seemed worth-while to use them as the basis of what, with little alteration, could be the pattern of our own local church organisation. Following the report's recommendation of five committees 'servicing' a central church Council, we now order our Group Council agenda under the following heads: Pastoral Work, Worship and Fellowship, Education and Youth, Stewardship and Finance, Citizenship and Social Service, Mission and Evangelism. 'Worship and Fellowship' is our own addition; 'Mission and Evangelism' we find are largely comprehended under the preceding five heads, but the inclusion of this item allows for the consideration of new evangelical enterprises

[13] *Op. cit.*, N. B. Cryer, Mowbray 1967, page 128.

and the over-all direction of our work. Much of the substance of the Group agenda is illustrated in the pages of this book.

The truth which emerges for us is that there is *no point* at which our existing church structures need be, or can remain, unrelated to mission and unity. Such major church committees as those reflected in our Group agenda can be related to ecumenical activities, or themselves become fully ecumenical bodies, just as and when this becomes appropriate in the given situation. The astonishing thing is that this is entirely possible even as we maintain our denominational identity. A small adjustment to a familiar agenda, a willingness to consult, report and listen, is all that is so often required to make possible the discovery of ourselves in the local situation as Christian colleagues. The 'new spirit' needs a renewed structure to breath through, and it is not beyond the capacity of any church to create it.

9. In Worship

IT may be that we have least to contribute to the greatest subject. But we believe that there is only one place where God's People are one—with the fullness of meaning which eludes our present understanding—and that is 'before God'.[1] It has been said that 'Christian Worship derives from two sources, the Jewish Synagogue and the Upper Room.'[2] To these sources of our worship we would wish to add the 'Mount' or the 'Temple'. If ancient Israel ever knew unity it was when encamped 'before the mount'[3]; if she aspired to unity it was through return to the Temple.[4] We believe that this dimension of worship is important to the true understanding of Christian unity, and that it is not sufficient for the local congregation to lay claim to its place within the One, Holy, Catholic and Apostolic Church, without making any attempt to realise (at the local level) the vision of the worship which transcends 'nation and tribe and tongue'.[5] The reader will judge how far we have ourselves fumbled and failed to make the vision recognisable. What we have to tell we introduce with another quotation from the Second Ecumenical Work Book—about prayer.

'Prayer is essential and fundamental Christian work. It means no longer merely confronting one another in our several traditions; nor even confronting the world in its opportunity and need; but being (so to speak) side by side on our knees before God, being *open* to him as we identify

[1] See also Bible references, Chapter 2, page 15ff.
[2] *A Book of Worship compiled for the use of Congregationalists*, Introduction, page 8. O.U.P. 1948.
[3] Exod. 19:2, etc.
[4] Isa. 2:2-3, etc. Psalm 122:4.
[5] Rev. 7:9, etc.

ourselves with the prayer and the longing of Christ himself "that they may all be one, that the world may believe" . . . That it is beginning to happen is surely due, in no small measure, to the increased volume and urgency of such prayer even during the last four or five years—and not least during the Week of Prayer for Christian Unity each January.'[6] All this is true. No one in our situation would want to deny for a moment the importance of the years that have passed in which the fullest possible use was made, in January, Holy Week or periods of special Joint Mission, of special acts of united prayer and public worship. That they have contributed here as elsewhere to the creation of a deeper awareness of Christ's will for us is not to be doubted. And yet . . . it has not seemed to us as the years have gone on that we can really hope to gain very much by restricting the progress of local reconciliation to special and specific acts of United Prayer at this or that season of the year. All too often it has seemed to us that Christians in some areas are too satisfied with the assertion that local unity is developing well when all that is being done in the way of local united worship is the same unchanging observance of the January week of prayer. In all too many places we have been aware, as at one stage amongst ourselves, of a false sense of sobriety and security, as if the occasional exchange of pulpits and the well-organised round of prayer meetings at one denominational centre after another in the evenings of the January Octave were the very acme of local ecumenical worship.

For us this has ceased to be an adequate objective. We begin to see united work of prayer and praise arising out of what we ARE in the other spheres of our common activity and encounter. Here are two examples:

In Chapter 7 we provided outlines of three of the important lay conferences which have been such a spur to our common

[6] *Op cit.*, page 8.

thinking and action. As the second conference came round the issue of what kind of worship ought to be observed at its close also came up for discussion. At the invitation of the Bishop of Croydon the ministers of the churches from which delegates would come met and considered the matter in detail. The Bishop made clear that there was no difficulty from the Anglican side about a joint act of Communion provided that this could be shown to have arisen from a serious intention for unity and from a common desire among the people concerned. The ministers reported that there had already been requests for such a closing act on the Saturday evening but it was eventually accepted that such a service would cause misgiving to some—particularly among those new to this experience of ecumenical fellowship. In view of these misgivings and in the knowledge that half the delegates would be attending for the first time, it was decided not to press the point but to put it to the conference members for their consideration when they prepared for the third conference the year afterwards. This was duly done. The second conference closed with an agreed form of evening devotions in the host church and the conference members went away with the issue of what should be the form of closing worship the next year as one to be discussed and resolved during the following months.

In the event the decision was virtually unanimous for the third year. There would be a celebration of the Holy Communion according to the Anglican rite, the Bishop being the celebrant, and all communicant members amongst the delegates were invited to share in the communion as full members. The fourth year saw the conference held in the Shirley Methodist Church and the communion on that occasion was conducted by the local Methodist minister, according to a 'free' order, the congregation remaining seated for the reception of the elements. This, it would now seem, is the natural pattern for closing these important occasions, when for most of the day the delegates have been consciously and seriously in 'fellowship', seeking to draw more closely together but not forgetting their continual need for a grace which must come ultimately from 'on high' and cannot be found in their own strivings. Whether this is a pattern for imitation in the present seeming impasse of the Anglican-Methodist debate is for others more knowledgeable to consider. For us at any rate it has seemed wise to allow 'intercommunion' to 'grow out of' a situation rather than to be imposed upon it. In practice the Addiscombe churches already enjoy a wide freedom in this matter.

Another example might be taken from the encounter of Christians in the Home Fellowships mentioned in Chapter 4. We are not here referring to the 'home communions' which have developed from the same instinct as within the lay conferences. We refer to something rather different. During the years 1961–4 the Parochial Church Council of St. Mary's had constantly been considering the practice and local discipline regarding Infant Baptism. Two public meetings were held at which this and other matters of public worship were debated and new procedures inaugurated. It was the advent of the Home Fellowships however which brought a new light to bear upon the matter of Infant Baptism. Several of the Anglican members of these groups had both heard of and witnessed the Methodist form of Infant Baptism—at a public service, the parents making due response, the congregation being committed to care for these children, and the whole act related to the general life and membership of the local Society. This could not but impress the Anglicans and it was as a direct result of this kind of exchange of knowledge and practice that from 1964 onwards the same general principles were introduced into the baptismal practice at St. Mary Magdalene's. In a very real sense the manner of conducting infant baptism at the neighbouring churches has become well-nigh identical and any attempt to slip from one church to the other 'for less fuss' has been plainly, though we also hope, gently prevented.

Worship for us then has gradually become a matter of proper co-ordination and assimilation so that together we have been able to present to the 'people next door' a sense of common purpose and identity which would not belie what they saw us attempting in each other's homes or on Wednesdays at the Community Night centre. For this very reason we have encouraged the idea of bringing our young people together on certain Sunday evenings in one church or another. Not in order to attempt some odd kind of service as a gimmick, though some of the special services arranged by the young people themselves have been outstanding examples of 'real holiness in words and action' but so that the next generation shall never feel out of place as they move with each other into previously unknown types of religious expression. Neville has been urged to record that this has not been done without sacrifice. When the Anglican young people joined their neighbours for such a service the choir of the Parish Church was almost wholly depleted! Again, the lay conference on one occasion recommended that in the coming autumn the groups of delegates should go in turn on successive Sunday evenings to the different churches represented by each group's members. This plan was carried out with great goodwill and the education imparted to the participants, quite apart from the effect on a congregation of knowing that they were being 'visited', was considered to have been tremendously worthwhile.

In much the same way there has now been a greatly valued step forward in regard to our Roman Catholic neighbours. At first and before Vatican II it was the custom for a few of the Anglicans, with their Vicar, to attend at Mass on some of the mornings in the week of Prayer for Unity, but this was only a gesture. In 1964 Ministers of the local Anglican and

Methodist churches were present by invitation at the dedication of the new Roman Catholic church in Bingham Road. The places of honour and the welcome accorded them on that occasion could leave the congregation in no doubt as to the significance attached by Bishop (now Archbishop) Cowderoy of Southwark to their presence. We were glad to be there and could not share the fears of ultra-Protestants that we were thus betraying Protestant convictions or encouraging misconceptions amongst our Roman Catholic neighbours.

For some four years now they have been permitted and willing to share a common act of worship in the Unity Prayer Octave and indeed the priority given to this evening in that week has meant that the attendance from all the churches has been noteworthy. More than that, however, we have now had three annual Scout and Guide services on a joint basis, the 1967 service taking place in the Roman Catholic Church with Neville sitting in the sanctuary and conducting the final prayers as well as delivering the benediction. For many of the boys and girls this has taken them across a barrier which even for our generation seemed likely to be still insurmountable. What is much more to the point is that we have tried to rescue joint worship from two of its otherwise real dangers. The unreality of keeping it to set times of the year only, and the artificiality of using only 'specially prepared' forms of service. We have wanted to introduce people to the real worship of their neighbours and to the kind of devotional activity in which they each live and move and have their being. It is this which needs to be fostered and exchanged far more than it still is. If we have one particular joy it is in having been able to achieve this so far as has been possible—but there is still plenty of ground to be covered!

For there *are* limits as we are only too well aware. Some months ago a young air-hostess who had been prepared for confirmation in 1964 by Neville came to him with the news that she was soon hoping to be married. She wanted him to share her good news even though she could not ask him to marry them since the man she was to marry had divorced his wife some years ago. What she did want from Neville was advice as to where she could possibly be married locally. Neville suggested that she should contact Ernest, explaining the circumstances but recognising that in Methodism it was not the case of divorced persons being married in Church automatically. After hearing their case Ernest was able to welcome the couple in due course to the Addiscombe church and Neville also received his invitation to the wedding—an invitation gladly accepted. For this girl and her husband (both of whom now regularly attend church together) our co-operation and colleagueship had kept the church in perspective for them both. We had not destroyed any laws—but we had somehow revealed a common Lord in our ministry.

In the same way there has been a healthy and still legal development in regard to our presence at services of confirmation and reception into full membership. The mere fact that the ordained minister of the neighbouring congregations has been in attendance when men and women, boys and girls, have stepped into a position of responsible stewardship within the Christian Church has been recognised and appreciated by many people. No comment has more weighed with Neville than that following his first appearance at a Reception service in the Methodist Church at Addiscombe where he was invited to extend the right hand of fellowship to all those who were taking part. One parent came to him at the meal afterwards and said, 'Oh, if only we had been able to experience this when we were received into membership. Our son does appreciate it!' If such a remark is a *skandalon* to the theologian it is manna to a caring pastor.

Mention has already and rightly been made about the joint services for the elderly and the appreciation which is felt for this kind of co-operative work on a Saturday morning. The welcome which the minister receives, whoever he may be, is utterly genuine and—quite apart from the economy of time and effort which this kind of service represents for the ministers and the organisers—it also brings to the people who attend the widest kind of ministry which they could hope to have. They hear the Gospel in its different shades and with its special presentations—indeed a truly 'Catholic' gospel.

A similar impulse lay behind the form of healing ministry which flourished here in the years 1965 and 1966. This is not the place to spell out in detail the history and background of the healing ministry in Addiscombe for that is a story which deserves a life of its own. Suffice it to say that since the war and up to 1964 there had been a steady healing ministry exercised in the Parish of St. Mary Magdalene and only the departure of the assistant curates meant that for a time this ministry had to be curtailed. In 1965 however, God brought to Addiscombe a Christian couple, Norman and Gwen Slade. For them the ministry of healing was one of God's blessings and one of the Church's neglected gifts. Here, in fruitful soil, they sought once more to re-establish the ministry which had continued before. This time, however, it was to be on a united basis.

The invitation to the services was made as wide and as informal as possible and after a short while we were offered the use of the Methodist Church also for the alternate occasions in the month. In order not to overburden Neville the services were led by ministers from various churches or the chaplains of Christian healing homes and again the same richness and variety was able to invade this common worship and shared ministry. Moreover, the fact that the services were not always in the Parish church permitted the widest possible range of healing ministry. The laying-on-of-hands by authorised persons was not the only form employed. Sometimes there would be 'anointing', and in the Methodist Church there could be 'open' communion.[7] Sometimes there would be a more formal service of readings, confession, absolution, address and hymns. On other occasions there would be silence, guided meditation, extempore prayers, calls for special help and a soloist. Again there was the same willing help from people who acted as chauffeurs, people who sent out invitations and people who made the tea-meal which always followed the services. The Slades were the inspiration behind it all, arranging the speaker or minister, sending out the quarterly prayer paper, organising the transport and keeping up to date the 'Silver Book' (a list of persons specially asking for prayer) which was kept in the interval between the services in an honoured place in the Parish Church sanctuary. We mention this here to emphasise yet again how we have sought, deliberately and consciously, to make our common worship more than a thing of special or peculiar importance. It has been our concern and, even more, our delight to see united worship touch young and old, the hale and the infirm, the occasional and the regular worshipper—in short to make our worship as united, though not as uniform, as it could possibly be within the bounds that official separation requires that it remain.

At the point of prayer and intercession the life of our churches has been brought especially close. The congregations of St. Mary Magdalene and the two Methodist Churches have long been accustomed to making local churches, their ministers and their work the subjects of their regular intercession. This has become as natural a part of worship as prayer for 'our own' congregation, or 'our own' missionaries, and it includes loving remembrance of ALL churches in the ecclesiastical spectrum. In a more intimate and personal way prayer for

---

[7] 'Open' here means as usual that recognised 'communicants' were welcome. It does not mean 'open to all and sundry'.

'Our Vicar' is naturally linked with prayer for 'Our Minister' in the weekly Methodist Prayer Fellowship and similarly in the Fellowship of the homes. This we see, more than all else, as the fruit of many years of growing in mutual respect, understanding and love.

One isolated occasion proved of significance for the Churches in Addiscombe. This was the 'continuous' reading of Mark's Gospel, the Acts, Pastoral Epistles and Revelation in December 1964, in association with the 'Feed the Minds' campaign. Throughout the day the Methodist Church was the scene of quiet meditation as readers and listeners came and went. This, we also believe, was the beginning of active association with the Christian Brethren and a time when denominational boundaries seemed particularly irrelevant—and non-existent.

There is still much to attempt however and much that at our best we would long to have attained. Let us list these briefly.

There is the whole issue of Lenten mid-week services. Already we have tried to show that progress in the home fellowships and Community Night has only been possible for us by making such sacrifices as will enable suburban worshippers and church-members to know where they might place their priorities. Thus the first week of the month had to be shorn of other adult activities so that people could go naturally to the united fellowship meetings. As we have seen, the Men's Forum surrendered its own identity in order to avoid an unrealistic call on men to come out on yet another evening. It was not until 1968 that we succeeded in relating the traditional Anglican Lenten Devotions to the pattern of our united activity. During the period elapsing between Neville's departure from St. Mary Magdalene and the coming of his successor, David Banfield, a Parish prayer group was formed, meeting on Tuesdays—the night of the Prayer Fellowship at the Addiscombe Methodist Church. For six successive Tuesdays in Lent 1968 the two prayer groups combined and sixty to seventy people shared in devotions based upon Bible study led by the Ministers, Church Army Captain and Diocesan Lay Reader. The experiment led to the request that a similar uniting of the two groups be arranged for Advent and, if possible, at one other period in the year. The desire to retain the intercessory nature of the groups, in which a great number of people are personally remembered, made it impracticable for them to unite on a permanent basis, but a firm relationship had been established.

There is also the matter of the Sundays of 'Parish Worship' to which passing reference has been made. Just because we were wanting to break away from formalised 'Unity services' or special seasons of Prayer for Unity we decided in 1965 that we could no longer keep our acts of joint worship to January alone. Rather should we seek to express our growing together in acts of common worship which would become *normal* to the life of our churches. Accordingly we have been holding 'Parish Worship' with the combined congregations in the parish church (as the only building capable of holding the 500 to 600 people involved) on two occasions in the year. On one occasion we would have the service of Morning Prayer and on the other the Methodist minister would conduct the service according to the local form in the Methodist Church.

A significant feature of these services is that no one now asks that they be held on a 'neutral' ground. In January 1965 the now largely disused building of the former Congregational Church was carefully prepared for us and provided a dignified centre for a 'Methodist' parish service. We no longer feel justified in this kind of artificiality. It is now accepted that 'Parish Worship' is held in the Parish Church.

These have proved to be stirring occasions—but they have their problems. Despite the wish of all to make them a complete manifestation of what we would envisage as the 'Parish

Family' of the future, the junior departments of the Methodist Sunday School have felt that they could not yet, or at least on more than one occasion, bring their scholars to the Parish Church on these Sundays. We all understand their perfectly legitimate reasons for this but the effect is to debar some families from enjoying what the rest of us are seeking and, we trust, finding. No one can see or expect an easy answer. All that one can see and know is that here in plain facts are the issues that have to be wrestled with when the whole matter of 'joint worship' is conceived of.

Nor should we overlook the combining of our Church choirs on occasions for Joint Festivals of Music. We are fortunate in having at St. Mildred's a notable organ and a long tradition of fine music. Here we have found a natural centre for festivals of reading and singing, and organists and choirmasters have worked willingly together to make this possible. On Good Friday evening 1968, choirs from Anglican, Methodist and Roman Catholic churches contributed to a united service of readings and music; the congregation far exceeded the church's normal seating capacity. Such spontaneous uniting of the talents of several churches has about it the true spirit of thanksgiving and praise. The joy of these occasions seems to authenticate what biblical precedent and theological conviction would suggest to us, that within the life of the Christian Church in each place there needs to be a Worship, transcending the life of the local congregation, comparable with the festivals of ancient Judaism, linking us in spirit with the Temple worship of the first Christian generation and anticipating 'the great multitude which no man can number . . . standing before the throne and before the Lamb'.[8]

[8] Rev. 7:9.

10. In the Future

WE have already trespassed on the topics which might properly be dealt with here in what was said in the closing section of the last chapter. Already we can see whole areas of concern and involvement in which we hope that the years ahead will bring new insight and advance. We do not pretend that every major problem has been solved and all that remains to be done is to balance the account. It may well be that there now needs to be a period of consolidation. Our hope is that what has been begun may not only last but so "form" the lives and "inform" the minds of the next generation that they in their turn will taste the fruits of this 'experiment in unity' and achieve that local reconciliation which continues to elude so many.

Looking into the future for us, however, means starting with that other section of the Nottingham report entitled, 'All in each place'.[1] It begins by inviting the member churches of the B.C.C. to 'covenant together to work and pray for the inauguration of union by a date agreed amongst them' and then continues to 'dare to hope' that the date 'should not be later than Easter Day 1980'. By now it need hardly be stated that we, with those who first drew up this resolution, 'believe that we should offer obedience to God in a commitment as decisive as this'. To quote from a book published in 1966 and entitled, *A.D. 1980*,[2] 'All that is required of us is the steady will to unite. This will must work not only amongst ecclesiastical leaders but also in the local churches . . . Which local churches in Britain will be the first to apply the principle of

[1] Nottingham, Section 5A, paragraphs 1 and 2.
[2] See Bibliography.

target dates effectively to the unification of their own local mission, worship and training programmes? . . . The effect of such achievements will be incalculable on the movement of the churches towards reunion by 1980.'

To conclude the Nottingham resolutions at this point, 'Since unity, mission and renewal are inseparable we invite the member churches to plan jointly so that all in each place may act together forthwith in common mission and service to the world.' That is our agenda for the days ahead and the perspective narrowed down to our own area would appear to resolve into six specific areas of concern.

The first has already been touched on and concerns the permission to local churches to provide for the richest possible liturgical expression of our churches' common life. As with many other spheres of progress this step will involve the official leaders of our respective denominations and it is precisely at such a point as this that the whole significance of 'experimental areas' must be seen to lie. Is it possible that our kind of situation may have something relevant to say about the official negotiations at this juncture? At the moment there is continuing doubt and uncertainty as to exactly how to devise a service of Reconciliation in which those who have been episcopally ordained and those who have not may be so authorised to exercise their new ministries that on the one hand they may be henceforth acknowledged to be fully acceptable to the members of both churches whilst on the other hand there is to be no suggestion of re-ordination. We dare not presume to have more wisdom than those to whom is committed the resolution of this apparently insoluble paradox. What we do hope may be a consideration is the opportunity of areas such as our own being permitted to enjoy 'intercommunion' and common worship *de temps en temps* without any formal service such as the former at all. If we are wrong then time will reveal the flaws in the undertaking; if on the other hand real fruit for good emerges then perhaps the evidence of the working of the Spirit 'in the churches' may be taken more fully into account in the plans and deliberations of the future. Call this pragmatism if you like—it is interesting to discover how often such a proceeding reveals itself in the pages of the New Testament.[3]

Our second area of concern for the future must be with the place and nature of evangelism in our common life. We already see the Church's mission active in the Home Fellowships, the House Visiting, the opening of the Church's premises to the community and in the service rendered increasingly in partnership with others, but we sense the danger that the pragmatism for which we have pleaded might lose the distinctive insights of the Christian Gospel in mere public spiritedness. Our pre-occupation in recent years with other categories of mission has so far left us without the impetus or resources to share in a once much-talked-of mission to children, or in a more recent mission to youth sponsored by the Christian Brethren. Yet a controlling purpose of the call to reconciliation among Christians is that they might the better undertake their mission—'that the world might believe'. This is a continuing charge on the Christian Church, here as in any other part of the world, and it will only be this recognition, the wrestling with its implications and the forging of some common mind about it, that will bring the most likely and pleasing answer to God's call to us.

The third field of advance will then have to be in education. There are signs already that, due to the encouraging lead given by the British Lessons Council, there is a real possibility of arriving at an agreed curriculum for the departments which are involved in children's Christian education. The linking of the youth work, if it is logically pursued, will involve some kind of common policy there in regard to instruction, as and

[3] See Acts 5: 38, 39; 10: 47.

when it is possible to offer it. The opportunity of sharing in the preparation of young couples before marriage takes the process on another stage.

It still remains true that the preparation of adults for membership, the oversight of what is undertaken in the Home Fellowships, the training in greater depth of group leaders and lay readers or preachers, the relating of faith to employment or family living, and probably other facets of adult education not here recorded are all spheres in which closer and closer co-operation in the future would be invaluable. If, as has been suggested, we can make the fullest use of the insights revealed by *Clinical Theology* and Christian Teamwork then there is a very promising future before the churches in this part of the world. We shall be producing mature and well-informed Christians who will know how to live with each other and, much more important, how to create relationships with those who at present are outside the scope of the existing Church fellowships. We shall even be able to offer a supply of people with leisure and skill for the growing number of voluntary welfare services that a modern urban community decidedly requires.

A fourth direction for the days ahead must lead us into more effective relationship with our overseas and immigrant neighbours. No one pretends, least of all the authors, that we have begun to do more than scratch the surface of this increasingly significant factor in an area such as ours. The fact that in our time together there has developed in Croydon an International Committee, directly charged with the oversight of this kind of issue in the Borough, does not in any way relieve each part of the borough from its own direct responsibility. Here again, it is only as the churches work together that they can hope to serve a community whose composition is in daily process of change. Though there is now very little 'new' immigration, the number of our immigrant neighbours increases with the arrival of relations and fiancées and the incidence of a higher than average birthrate. Addiscombe, furthermore, offers a desirable improvement in housing conditions as compared with other inner London areas and there is evidence of a steady movement outwards from such districts as Brixton to Croydon. We already note the emergence of 'immigrant concentrations'.

It will be the special task of Christians in the streets and homes to decide just how they are going to react to this new social factor—to the 'people next door'. This is a matter which has only begun to be aired in a few Home Fellowships; it is going to be important to bring into much more extensive dialogue those of the new immigrant families who can make articulate, plainly and lovingly, the tensions and outlook which are theirs. There will have to be dialogue—and then more dialogue—before there can be any hope of making progress in this field. What, it is hoped, will not occur is that this issue will either be bypassed by the churches or left to the tender mercies of a few saintly individuals. The one move will be dangerous; the other will be totally inadequate.

Which brings us to the fifth piece of possible future development: the relationship between the churches and the so-called secular society in which it is set and in which the church member lives and works and finds part, at least, of his recreation. One would expect to see some distinctive part being played by the churches together in the many-sided life of a great municipality such as ours. These expectations will partly depend for their fulfilment upon the seriousness with which the local churches regard the work done by Miss Dorothy Cornwall as their liaison officer between the Churches and the Welfare agencies. If this essential link is to be maintained her successor may need, ultimately, to be a salaried officer serving a partnership of say six churches. But there are questions which go beyond any such appointment. Are the churches going to produce the M.P.s, the councillors, the school governors, the trades union officials, the Chamber of Commerce and other professional representatives? Here is a great opportunity for the Christians in an area to present their convictions through their representatives and in turn to be kept abreast of all that is going on in the essential framework of modern city dwelling. It can never be enough for the members of Christ's body to be involved in their own mutual reconciliation or the private reconciliation of individuals to their God. It must be the common work of the Christians together in an area such as this to begin to affect public opinion, not by mounting a single political party, even if that were conceivable, or by seeking to organise pressure groups, but at least by providing men and women of conviction and 'grace-ful' personality who can speak and act with the knowledge that they do so with the prayers and insights of other local Christians behind them. They will find, as the representatives of the British Council of Churches find, that Governments and public bodies will treat Christian opinion all the more seriously when they know that those who speak to them do so in the name and with the backing of a united group of Christian churches.

The sixth area of concern is the realistic and strategic use of property and plant. Already each of the churches has got problems concerning the most economical use of existing structures, and the way in which the Oval Road premises are being planned for use in the future should give us heart to weigh with care the use to which the other parts of the ecclesiastical buildings can best be put. Already St. Mary Magdalene's P.C.C. have considered a possible re-organisation of their whole church interior so as to give the church a new liturgical look and make more rooms available for instructional and recreational work. Is not the time fast approaching when a strategy for church building development will have to be worked out among the Addiscombe churches, with a willingness to help each other, both with ideas and cash, in making the premises of all the churches one great complex of maximum benefit to all? It is a daunting and far from simple prospect; yet it is the magnitude of the task and not its undesirability which is perhaps the greatest deterrent to a start being made. It is a task for the future indeed and one that will require humility, foresight, frankness and commitment on the part of the churches' leaders. Without it there could be the wasting of energy and resources which no local area can afford.

We are aware that, in describing the 'experiment', we may have begged the issue of 'unity'. The reader may reasonably ask what shape of church is likely to emerge from the principles of mutual recognition and 'working together' which we have both enunciated and attempted to put into practice. We have no definitive answer. While we cannot conceive of a unity which is formless, we find ourselves partly at odds with those who seem most concerned to impress the 'correct' ecclesiastical and theological forms upon us. We believe that forms are important, but not as important as attitudes, and in attitudes we do not find ourselves or our 'ecumenical' friends guiltless: the unity Christ wills does not shut doors on others simply because others shut doors on us. The capacity to shift denominational mole-hills into an ecumenical mountain, 'without love', will achieve nothing. Our hope and prayer is simply that, as the 'churches' work together as far as they can, some shape or form will emerge which will make evident to the world our acknowledgement of one another as Christ's and our acknowledgement of God's purpose in Him for us all. We close with realistic words from the American New Testament scholar, John Knox:

'How confidently can we expect the coming great church? How likely is the achievement of the Christian unity we seek? If by "unity" we mean perfect harmony, the complete absence of differences in practice and opinion among Christians, identity of theological emphasis, absolute uniformity in worship, and the like, it is clear that such "unity" not only is impossible but ought not to be desired—that is, within history. We are not good enough or wise enough to be thus united; it would not do for us to agree perfectly with all others, as it certainly would not do for all others to agree perfectly with us. Only in heaven will there be this kind of peace, and only there would it be tolerable. But what shall we say of the possibility of our achieving a more feasible and appropriate kind of unity—a unity allowing for great freedom and many differences but expressing itself in a single visible body (like the body of a nation) to which all Christians would belong? Even this seems remote; our various divergent traditions are strong and our prejudices even stronger. Some of us find it almost impossible to give others the freedom they must have, and others find it just as hard to acknowledge any curb upon their freedom; or, to speak more accurately perhaps, both groups prefer the familiar curbs their own denominations impose to the necessarily more generous limits a universal church would prescribe. For actually what often repels us in the idea of the universal church is not the limitations it would place on us but the freedom it would give others—and this is true whether we be Protestant or Catholic . . .

'But this achievement when it comes will not be a human achievement. . . . Our part in the building will be allowing ourselves to be "built in", yielding ourselves without reservation—without care for a single vested interest, without self-righteous fidelity to a single ancient prejudice—to the mighty working of the Spirit, who alone can break down all dividing walls of hostility and can reconcile us all to God in one body.'[4]

[4] *The Early Church and the Coming Great Church*, John Knox. Epworth, 1957, pages 152–153.

Appendices

ABBREVIATIONS

B.C.C.	The British Council of Churches.
'Conversations'	Anglican-Methodist—The official report of Conversations between the Church of England and the Methodist Church, Epworth Press and Church Information Office, 1963. 3s. 6d.
L.M.	Leaders' Meeting. Body under chairmanship of Minister with oversight of local Methodist Society.
Lund	W.C.C. Conference on Faith and Order, held at Lund, Sweden, 1952.
'Nottingham'	The first British Conference on Faith and Order, held at Nottingham in September 1964: also used of the report 'Unity Begins at Home' which summarises the conference and provides the text of the resolutions.
P.C.C.	Parochial Church Council. Body providing for lay participation with incumbent in oversight of the local Anglican church.
P.N.D.	'The People Next Door' programme of study and action sponsored by the B.C.C. and the Conference of British Missionary Societies for use by Christians in Great Britain during the early part of 1967.
S.C.K.	The Servants of Christ the King.
W.C.C.	World Council of Churches. First Assembly, Amsterdam 1948. Subsequent Assemblies: Evanston, U.S.A., 1954; New Delhi, India, 1961; Uppsala, Sweden, 1968.

SOME ADDRESSES

Abbeyfield Society, 22 Nottingham Place, London, W.1.

The British Council of Churches, 10 Eaton Gate, S.W.1.

Clinical Theological Association, 'Lingdale', Weston Avenue, Mount Hooton Road, Nottingham.

Conference of British Missionary Societies, Edinburgh House, 2 Eaton Gate, London, S.W.1.

National Christian Education Council (formerly National Sunday School Union), Robert Denholm House, Nutfield, Redhill, Surrey.

(*Note that local branches may still use the title 'Sunday School Union'*)

National Council of Social Service, 26 Bedford Square, London, W.C.1.

Parish and People, 300 Granville Road, Sheffield, 2.

Servants of Christ the King, 225 Archway Road, London, N.6.

World Council of Churches, 150 Route de Ferney, 1211 Geneva 20, Switzerland.

(*Note that W.C.C. publications are all available through B.C.C.*)

SHORT BIBLIOGRAPHY

A list of selected publications and pamphlets on the ecumenical movement is available from the Publications Department, B.C.C.

Introduction

The following studies of ecumenical history are recommended:

The Ecumenical Movement, Norman Goodall. O.U.P. 21s.

The Age of Disunity, John Kent. Epworth. 35s.

Church Unity Without Uniformity, Harold Wood. Epworth. 35s. (A study of seventeenth century English Church movements)

The Church and Christian Union, Bampton Lectures 1964, Stephen Neill. O.U.P. 1968.

Chapter 1

General

The British Churches Today, Kenneth Slack. S.C.M., 1961. 5s.

A Study of Church Life in Britain, K. A. Busia. World Studies of Churches in Mission, 1967. 21s.

Centres of Renewal (The life of the lay institute in Europe). W.C.C. 6s.

Living Springs, Olive Wyon. S.C.M.. 8s. 6d. [Out of print.]

Star Books on Reunion (By joint Anglican-Methodist authors). Mowbray and Epworth. 3s. 6d. (5 titles). [Out of print.]

From local situations

Parishes with a Purpose, N. B. Cryer. Mowbray, 1967. 8s. 6d.

News From Notting Hill, Mason, Ainger and Denny. Epworth, 1967. 6s.

Areas of Ecumenical Experiment, R. M. C. Jeffery. B.C.C. 6s. (Including Corby, Blackburn Leys, Halewood, Crowborough)

New Area Mission, Trevor Beeson. Mowbray, 1964. 8s. 6d.

Chapter 2

Unity Begins at Home, The 'Nottingham' Report. S.C.M. 3s. 6d.

Visible Unity—What does the Bible Say?, J. M. Ross. B.C.C. 1s. 6d.

The Bible and Unity, R. E. Davies. B.C.C. 9d.

New Delhi Speaks, Official reports from the 1961 Assembly on Witness, Service and Unity. S.C.M. 2s. 6d.

Second Ecumenical Work-Book, Programme suggestions for local Councils. B.C.C. 1s. 6d.

Growing Together Locally, Revised 1965. B.C.C. 1s.

Baptists For Unity, 1968. Available from 69 Oldfield Road, Coventry. 1s. 6d.

Anglican-Methodist Unity. Report of the Anglican-Methodist Unity Commission. Part 2. The Scheme. S.P.C.K. and Epworth Press. 1968. 10s. 6d.

All in Each Place, Ed. J. I. Packer. Marcham Books, 1965. 18s.

The Body of Christ, Alan Cole. Hodder and Stoughton, 1964. 3s. 6d.

Religious Sociology, A. F. Boulard. Darton Longman & Todd, 1959.

The Church's Understanding of Itself, R. H. T. Thompson. S.C.M., 1957.

Chapter 3

The Church in Your House, John Banks. Epworth, 1966. 5s.

Groups—See how they Run, John Banks. Epworth, 1967. 2s. 6d.

The Dynamics of the Small Group. Clinical Theological Association. See Addresses.

Home Meetings. Christian Advance Training Course. Leaflet 2/1. Church Army. 6d.

Chapters in:

Laity Studies 2–6 (The Church in the House). W.C.C. 8s.

Like a Mighty Army, A. P. Wood. (The Englishman's Home.) Marshall, Morgan and Scott. 8s. 6d.

Living Room Dialogues, ed. by Wm. B. Greenspun and Wm. A. Norgren. N.C.C.C. and Paulist Press. Available from B.C.C. 9s.

Chapter 4

Training in Visitation, Lewis Misselbrook. Baptist Union Publications. 2s. 6d.

To Everyman's Door, M. A. P. Wood. Church Pastoral Aid Society. 1s. 6d.

Visiting. Christian Advance Training Course. Leaflet 1/3. Church Army. 6d.

Chapter 5

Where in the World?, Colin W. Williams. Epworth. 6s. 6d. (A study of the missionary structure of the congregation following the 'call' of the New Delhi Assembly.)

The Church for Others, Two reports on the missionary structure of the congregation. W.C.C. 9s. 6d.

God's Frozen People, Gibbs and Morton. Fontana, 1964. 3s. 6d.

Christian Unity in Sheffield, Martin Reardon. B.C.C. 2s. 6d.

Areas of Ecumenical Experiment, R. M. C. Jeffery. B.C.C. 6s.

[See Desborough, pp. 7–15 and Appendix.]

APPENDICES

Chapter 6

Consumer's Guide to the British Social Services, Phyllis Willmott. Pelican. 6s.

Christians and Social Work, Kathleen Heasman. S.C.M.

What in the World?, Colin W. Williams. Epworth. 6s. 6d. (A study of the relationship of the Church and the World.)

Church and Society, Report of the W.C.C. Conference, July 1966. W.C.C. 10s. 6d.

Responsibility in the Welfare State?, A Study of relationships between the Social Services and the Churches in a City suburb. Birmingham Council of Churches. B.C.C. 5s.

The World is the Agenda, Ed. Trevor Beeson. Parish and People.

Dialogue with the World, J. G. Davies. S.C.M. 4s. 6d.

The Caring Community, National Council of Social Service. 3s.

Partnership in Ministry, Ed. Trevor Beeson. Mowbray, 1964. 9s. 6d.

The Caring Church, Ed. Peter Smith. Peter Smith Ltd., 1964. 5s.

Chapter 7

The majority of the books and pamphlets listed in this bibliography provide material for inter-church study. We particularly draw the attention of the reader to W.C.C. and B.C.C. Reports, which are issued to enable the local church to share in and contribute to the thinking of its ecumenical representatives. Amsterdam, Evanston, New Delhi, Uppsala, Lund and Nottingham, have no fundamental significance for the life of the Church until they have been translated into the terms and experience of the Church in each locality.

Chapter 8

The Ordained Ministry

News from Notting Hill, Formation of a Group Ministry (A Methodist Experiment), Mason, Ainger and Denny. Epworth, 1967. 6s.

The Shape of the Ministry, Report 1965. B.C.C. 3s.

Team Ministries, Report of a working party to the Methodist Conference 1967. Epworth. 1s.

Planning for Mission, Ed. T. Weiser. Epworth. 12s. 6d.

Church Government, Levett and Rogers. ('Star Books', Mowbray and Epworth). 3s. 6d.

The Laity

The Role of the Diakonia in Contemporary Society, Report to W.C.C. Conference. W.C.C. 6s. 6d.
Laity, Five studies. W.C.C. 6s.
The Ministry of Deacons, Studies No. 2. W.C.C. 9s. 6d.

The W.C.C. has published a bibliography of over 1,000 items on the theme of the Laity.

Chapter 9

The Calendar and Lectionary, Recommendations of a joint Liturgical Group, Ed. R. C. D. Jasper. O.U.P., 1967. 7s. 6d.
One Lord. One Baptism, Studies in ministry and worship. S.C.M. 6s. [Out of print.]
Joining in Common Prayer, W. Nicholls. 'The Unity We Seek' study booklet. B.C.C. 2s.
Worship in a United Church, Beeson and Sharp. ('Star Books', Mowbray and Epworth.) 3s. 6d.
Worship and Mission, J. G. Davies. S.C.M. 8s. 6d.
That They May All be One, Five short services for Schools. B.C.C. 8d.
Unity in Christ, An Order of Service. B.C.C. 20s. per 100.

Chapter 10

The Early Church and the Coming Great Church. John Knox. Epworth, 1957. 12s. 6d.
A.D. 1980, A. H. Dammers. Lutterworth, 1966. 8s. 6d.
'The Holy Spirit and the Catholicity of the Church,' from: *Drafts for Sections*, Uppsala 1968. B.C.C. 8s. 6d.
Is Sacrifice Outmoded?, Kenneth Slack. S.C.M., 1966. 6s.
The Questioning Church, Cardinal Döpfner. Burns and Oates, 1964. 7s. 6d.
The Unfinished Task, Stephen Neill. Edinburgh House and Lutterworth, 1957. [Out of print.]

LIBRARY OF DAVIDSON COLLEGE

Books on regular loan may be checked out for
be presented at the   Desk in